Thoughts on Open Innovation

**Essays on Open Innovation from
leading thinkers in the field**

An OpenForum Academy publication

Thoughts on Open Innovation

Thoughts on Open Innovation

Table of Contents

Things To Come

Learn More

An introduction to
"Thoughts on Open Innovation"

By Karel De Vriendt

"If I have seen farther it is by standing on the shoulders of giants."
Sir Isaac Newton, 1676

Although the term "Open Innovation" is attributed to Prof. Henry Chesbrough, who used it in a book published in 2003, the concept is much older, as demonstrated by the quote of Sir Isaac Newton. Already in the 17th century, scientists all over Europe were in contact with each other, sharing the results of their experiments and the theories based on these results. Since then, collaboration and sharing has been the norm in scientific communities and limitations in the possibilities to do so – due to tensions or even wars between nations – have always been considered as hampering progress.

But, aside the "homo scientificus" for whom a better understanding of our world and sometimes also the potential advancement of humanity are sufficient drivers for devoting his life to science, there is also the "homo economicus", a rational person who's ultimate driver is self-interest. And, there is a widespread belief – at least as old as the idea of sharing and collaboration in scientific communities – that without proper protection to ensure that the inventor, via patents, has, for a limited period, exclusive rights on the usage of his/her invention, no rational person would invest in original work.

The "homo economicus", the rational thinking individual driven by self-interest is also at the basis of free market theories.

7

In many of these theories, free access to information and the absence of market-entry barriers are considered preconditions for real competition and it is real competition that ensures optimal use of natural, human and financial resources, generating maximum benefits for society as a whole. According to these theories, providing temporary monopolies to inventors is not needed, the rational homo economicus will also without such protection try to improve the goods or services he/she produces in order to gain a small, temporary advantage over the competition.

Back to "Open Innovation". When Prof. Chesbrough introduced the term, he was speaking about innovation strategies to be used by individual firms in order to gain a competitive advantage in the market. It is the recognition that no firm, however big it is, can only rely on internal innovation resources in our global world.

Today, "Open Innovation" has a broader meaning. It is part of a whole family of concepts that often share the word "open" and the concept of "openness".[1] Open Knowledge, Open Data, Open Source Software, Open Standards, Open Innovation but also the concepts behind the Creative Commons all are based on the same basic ideas: by collaborating with others, by re-using (and by being allowed to re-use) the results of the efforts of others and by allowing others to use and improve the results of our efforts, we all get better. We can use "Open Innovation" as a term encompassing most of the other "Open" things.

The debate is not only economical – is it beneficial for economical actors to be "more open"? – but also societal. While

---

[1]   The "European Interoperability Framework" (http://ec.europa.eu/isa/documents/isa_annex_ii_eif_en.pdf) defines openness as "the willingness of persons, organizations or other members of a community of interest to share knowledge and stimulate debate within that community, the ultimate goal being to advance knowledge and to use that knowledge to solve problems."

there is little doubt that more openness will be beneficial to society, how can we balance openness with the need of companies to stay competitive and to make a profit (to survive and to invest) and provide enough incentives to bright spirits to continue to innovate? Is openness an absolute good: should all knowledge, all data, all software, all standards, etc. be open or are there situations where openness should be avoided – maybe for reasons of security or privacy or for reasons of economical self-interest? How do we organise the involvement of as many individuals or organisations as possible in efforts to solve societal issues using Open Innovation? How do we organise Open Innovation projects and ensure that such project are, and remain, "Open"?

That is what this collection of essays is about.

The book starts with two essays that give the bigger picture: Andy Updegrove describes how knowledge was shared in the past and how the arrival of the Internet changed drastically the process of sharing and reusing knowledge, making openness a central concept in this process. And Shane Coughlan starts from the definition of "Open Innovation" as introduced by Prof. Henry Chesbrough and extends then the concept to cover the current practice.

The two following essays describe examples on how Open Innovation works in practice: Peter Murray-Rust and other volunteers from the Open Knowledge Foundation describe examples from areas as diverse as chemistry, self-help and libraries. Also the concept of the "citizen scientist" is introduced. Coleman McCormick describes the very successful OpenStreetMap project.

The next group of essays touches some of the most widely debated topics in the world of Openness: Jochen Friedrich writes about the "contradiction" between Openness and Intellectual Property Rights ("patents") in ICT standardisation. Karsten

Gerloff writes about current public procurement practices that are often unfavourable to the offering and the use of Open Source Software in public administrations but also about how some public administrations have successfully introduced Open Source Software. Amanda Brock writes about working with Open Source Software in a commercial world.

The book finishes with two essays of a more philosophical and visionary nature: Simon Phipps presents the problem of the position and the rights of the individual – as user and buyer but also as creator or collaborator – in a world where the rules are tailored towards the needs of large corporations. And finally, Peter Langley sees possibilities of a patent system that is more favourable to Open Source and all other things Open;

I hope that you enjoy reading the essays in this book but, more importantly, I hope that the book can contribute to an "Open" debate about "Open Innovation".

Karel De Vriendt worked twenty five years (1987-2012) as an IT expert for the European Commission. From 2005 to 2011, he was leading the team responsible for the implementation of the IDABC programme and for the definition and implementation of the ISA programme. He was actively involved in initiatives such as the transeuropean network TESTA, the Open Source Observatory and Repository (OSOR) and the SemanticInteroperability Centre Europe (SEMIC) now both merged into Joinup and in the elaboration of the European Interoperability Strategy and the European Interoperability Framework. During his career, he also acquired a good practical experience in the public procurement of IT goods and services. Karel De Vriendt is now retired but has kept his interest in improving (computer based) public services via the collaboration between public and private partners and via the sharing and re-use of software based service components. He also remains a big supporter of open standards and open source software as essential elements to support collaboration, sharing and reuse.

Thoughts on Open Innovation

Context

Thoughts on Open Innovation

"Openness" and the Pursuit of Knowledge

By Andrew Updegrove

Until the advent of the Internet, the acquisition of knowledge was a linear process, with the discoveries of one innovator only becoming available to be built upon by the next after being reported to, evaluated by, and eventually published in a journal of repute. Similarly, the process of creation of collaborative works was largely limited to individuals that were physically in one location, due to the need for real time communication. Not surprisingly, the legal rules, tools and practices that evolved over time reflected this sequential and insular process of creation, tilting the balance of rights towards the creators, in part because the opportunities for societally beneficial, real-time sharing were limited. Now that those limitations have fallen away, creators of all types are voluntarily relaxing their ownership rights in order to mutually enjoy the benefits of greater access, faster development, and more useful collaboration. In this article, I review some of the many ways and domains in which this revolution is occurring, highlight some of the legal tools that innovative individuals have created in order to facilitate this process, and offer thoughts on how these important developments in the acquisition and sharing of knowledge can best be encouraged to thrive in the future.

Throughout human history, the expansion of knowledge has been linear and accretive: in pre-history, individuals acquired and shared information, and to the limited extent possible passed that knowledge along to the next generation. But since knowledge could not be recorded, it was at constant risk of loss or corruption. Moreover, this dependence on oral transmission limited the complexity of knowledge that could be transmitted through the "lowest common denominator" of understanding of each human link in the chain. Impressive advances could be easily lost — as occurred 50,000 years ago, when the descendants of the first humans to reach Australia lost the technology to make sea voyages. Some of their descendants, settling on isolated islands off shore from their new home, even lost the ability to make fire.

The invention of writing crucially allowed knowledge to expand much more rapidly, since discoveries could now not only be preserved in faithful detail and built upon by others, but also shared more widely across both space and time. Moreover, because the peoples that used writing also lived in town-based, hierarchical societies, classes of people now existed with the desire and time to learn. With some of the best minds of the times now able to stand on the shoulders of their predecessors, and in turn "speak" to the best and the brightest of the next generation, the increasing pool of knowledge could be utilised to create much more complex types of learning based upon abstractions, through reasoning and inference. Wars and catastrophes could still set knowledge back dramatically within any single society, but with the dispersion of knowledge there was greater likelihood that some of the unique discoveries of one culture would be communicated to another, sustaining society linked through trade or alliance. The result of writing and communication was therefore that the preservation of knowledge had at last become less ephemeral, and the capacity to create new knowledge more robust.

Though the process of knowledge creation and preservation now led to great advances in complex disciplines such as mathematics, philosophy and astronomy, the process of advancement remained largely linear, slow, and accretive. This, because the utilisation of information beyond small communities of scholars remained mediated by the need to write down and then physically transport the results to those that might take the next intuitive leap. The use of Latin (in the West) and Arabic (in the Islamic world) facilitated the sharing of ideas across international borders, but the limited travel infrastructure of the day ensured that even this process remained painfully slow.

In the modern era, advanced transportation systems began to hasten knowledge exchange, as postal systems became more reliable and swift, and as more scholars and experts could travel farther and more frequently to exchange and debate the fruits of their research first hand. With the invention and deployment of modern voice-based telecommunications technologies, verbal exchanges of summarised data, if not detailed research, became possible as well.

While these changes were historically dramatic, their impact was evolutionary, rather than revolutionary, since the exchange of information between geographically separate researchers and thinkers in the same disciplines was still likely to be occasional and episodic, rather than constant and seamless. As a result, researcher B would usually not have full access to the discoveries of researcher A until A's research had been submitted, evaluated, edited and at length published in a scientific journal, unless both A and B happened to be in trusted, personal communication. Thus, while the fidelity and range of knowledge transmission increased, the cycle of its reuse remained painfully slow.

A less obvious limitation of the technologies of the times was the impracticality of assembling collaborative communities across distances that could work on the same projects simultaneously. Those with the knowledge and ability to achieve impressive results through collaboration were thus constrained to work in comparative isolation, sometimes unknowingly working on the same problems, and even conducting the same experiments, that others were tackling at the same time. This separation encouraged rivalry rather than collaboration, further inhibiting the free exchange of discoveries until primacy of discovery could be established through disclosure in a respected journal.

Similarly, the roles of research and development remained largely separate, in part because those trained in the exploitation of new ideas were not likely to be direct participants in the types of communities that engaged in pure research.

With the advent of the Internet and the Web and the increasing adoption in the wired world of English as a successor to Latin and Arabic, many of these age-old logistical constraints have fallen away. Today, it is possible for individuals from around the world to form communities large and small that are able to not only immediately share facts, research, insights and hard results, but work concurrently on the same projects as well. The benefits of such real-time access to valuable data has encouraged many in the scientific community to become more open in consequence. It has also allowed communities of like-minded individuals to form that could never have reached critical mass in the past, when the pool of similarly interested and skilled individuals from which such a community could be formed was limited to those in geographical proximity.

In this article, I will describe some of the ways in which both individuals as well as these new technically enabled communities are transforming the ways in which knowledge is acquired and shared. More importantly, I will explore how the promise of these Web-enabled processes is providing incentives to adjust traditional ideas regarding the proper balance to be struck between the intellectual property rights (IPR) of individual owners and those of collaborative communities and end users. Finally, I will review some of the new legal tools and organisational structures that have been created in order to more fully realise the revolution in knowledge sharing and advancement that modern telecommunications technologies make possible.

The Needs of Linear vs. Real-Time Processes

For most of historical times, there was no need for a legal system to protect IPR, because even if the labours of creation were great, the benefits to the creator were often low. For example, in the academic world, recognition as the originator of a discovery or theory conveyed status and opportunity, but that value could be secured simply by providing a means whereby recognition as the first to discover could be established. This could be accomplished through presentation of papers at meetings of scientific societies, and through publication in journals.

Where value was greater, as in the case of manufacturing processes, rights to practice inventions for many years was protected simply through secrecy, enforced either individually, or collectively, in guilds.

But as an industrial society began to take shape, greater profits could be lost if imitators unsaddled by the costs of research and development could swiftly and cheaply "knock off" the easily understood physical world inventions of the times. In the case of works of authorship, expanding literacy rates increased the market for written materials dramatically, a need which advances in printing technology easily satisfied. Predictably, literary piracy became rampant.

The result was the development in modern times of legal systems that were concerned primarily with protecting the rights of innovators, inventors and authors, as compared to competitors and consumers. Still, in the case of inventions and works of authorship, there was recognition that the benefits to society of unfettered use were sufficiently significant that the control granted to inventors and authors over their creations should be finite rather than perpetual, with the period of exclusive enjoyment to be somehow appropriate to the labor and creativity invested.

The rights given to creators and inventors among the various forms of intellectual property also took into account the unique characteristics of the works in question. In the case of patents and copyrights, limits were imposed on the duration of the owner's right to exclude others from free use of their invention, idea, or work. Patent rights were assigned the shortest period of enjoyment, because the scope of the protection is most broad, representing a state-granted monopoly to practice the concept of an invention, rather than to produce a single, specific implementation of the innovation.

The exclusive publication rights granted under copyright are much narrower, protecting only the actual expression of the author (e.g., the words themselves, as compared to the underlying ideas), and the duration of exclusivity protected by law was therefore permitted to be longer. But even in the case of a novel, poem or essay, law makers decided that unfettered republication rights must necessarily pass eventually into the public domain.[2] In contrast, it was deemed appropriate for the exclusive rights in a trademark or service mark to be perpetual, because the cost to society of granting such exclusive rights is low. Still, there are limitations on the specific words that can become a trademark or service mark,[3] and the rights secured by a mark are also limited to the domain in which the product or service is actually offered (e.g., computer software).

Over time, the laws that evolved to reflect this balancing of interests has become increasingly uniform throughout the world. This was achieved through the refinement and wide adoption of a succession of treaties that apply to the principle forms of intellectual property recognised at law today (copyright, trademark and patent). These international agreements that treaty parties conform their internal laws to the requirements of the treaty (e.g., the Berne Convention) and may also mandate the enforcement of those same laws against infringers (e.g., the

---

[2] The duration of a copyright depends in part on the nature of the work and other factors, and is additionally complicated with respect to individual works by changes to the copyright laws over the years. Most recently in the United States the duration of a copyright was lengthened by 20 years under The Copyright Extension Act. That legislation was responsive to the vigorous lobbying efforts of major content owners, and particularly of the Walt Disney Corporation, the owner of a certain iconic cartoon character that was in imminent danger of falling into the public domain. The Copyright Extension Act therefore stands out as one of the clearest examples of truly "Mickey Mouse legislation."

[3] For example, a trademark may not be merely "descriptive." Otherwise, a cutlery vendor (for example) might trademark a word such as "knife," leaving its competitors with no way to identify their own competing products. In contrast, a trademark may be "suggestive" of the nature or virtues of a product, allowing a knife to bear a trademark such as "Chef's Delight."

Agreement on Trade Related Aspects of Intellectual Property Rights (TRIPS), which is binding on members of the World Trade Organisation (WTO)).

In the main, this legal regime has served developed nations well, and emerging nations therefore generally fell in step as they joined the global economy, adopting the same legal concepts, and with time, becoming party to many of the same treaties. At the dawn of the Internet era, the IPR legal infrastructure could therefore be viewed as a comprehensive, relatively mature global system, well attuned to the slowly evolving realities, values and needs of the societies the framework had been created to serve.[4]

The legal framework we know today evolved to serve the needs of a physical world, however. Those active in the virtual world soon found that the licenses and practices that had developed in the past seemed too constraining to serve the types of activities in which they were now technically able to engage. For example, the ability to place works of authorship on line and allow them to be manipulated collaboratively from anywhere in the world presented both opportunities as well as new issues. Such behaviour had never before been contemplated in a world where single authors created complete works that were then referenced in the writings of later authors. Not surprisingly, copyright laws were in some respects at best unhelpful, and at worst limiting.

---

[4] "Relatively mature" does not mean "final." For example, the World Intellectual Property Organization (WIPO) Copyright Treaty was adopted on December 20, 1996. It has since been implemented in varying forms in signatory nations such as the United States (in the Digital Millennium Copyright Act, or DMCA) and in the European Union (in Directive 2001/29/ EC of the European Parliament and of the Council of 22 May 2001 on the Harmonization of Certain Aspects of Copyright and Related Rights in the Information Society). This evolutionary process will undoubtedly continue.

Moreover, some communities that began to form around Internet-enabled opportunities reached different conclusions about what should change, and how. This was due in part to the fact that the range of subject matter opportunities was so broad (e.g., computer code development versus scientific research), but also because the motivations of the individuals that most publicly framed the resulting dialogue varied widely as well. In many respects, this dialogue assumed the need and the justification to revise the traditional balancing of rights between IPR owners and IPR users.

The result has been a still-emerging, and often spirited, debate over whether existing IPR laws need to change. At the same time, there has been a dynamic process of reapplying existing laws in new and often imaginative ways, in order to adapt the existing rule set to meet the needs and opportunities of our increasingly on-line world without the need for amending underlying laws at all.

The Open Revolution

At the heart of this modern revolution in thinking is the concept of "openness." While this still-evolving term has come to mean different things in different contexts (and often even within the same context, depending upon who is providing the definition), at minimum it recognises that a greater good can be achieved through the simultaneous or early sharing of information than by keeping it secret until formal publication, in the case of research, or perpetually, in the case of source code or other technical information. Often, it also includes free and unrestricted rights of reuse, for some, or for all purposes. The methodologies and legal tools that have been created to achieve these goals are therefore directed at enabling a greater degree of visibility, access, and reusability than in the past.

The following is a sampling of some of the more prominent "open" methodologies and rule sets that have arisen in the wake of the digital revolution.

Free Software

The concept of "free software" was conceived by Richard Stallman in 1983, before the Internet became widely used by other than academics. As proposed by Stallman, the designation "free" refers to freedom of access and reuse rather than a requirement that such rights be conveyed at no cost (although in fact most such software is also made available free of charge).[5] This distinction underlines the fact that something new is at issue here, rather than the traditional concerns that copyright was intended to protect. Instead of seeking to protect rights of economic exploitation, the rules that apply to free software are intended to ensure what amounts to rights of common ownership, largely independent of economic motivations. As a result, these rules are intended to guarantee the rights to use, copy, study, modify, and to share the original and any modified versions of the software in question with others.

In a sense, the software code is considered to be less a work of authorship, than a collection of ideas that can be shared, evolved and built upon, just as knowledge and research has traditionally been shared in academic circles. Intriguingly, copyright law has been repurposed to help create licenses to assure this new set of goals. That said, it is important to note that the concept of free and open software relates to the rights of developers and

---

[5] Perhaps as a reflection of the settings in which revolutionary concepts are often conceived, this distinction is invariably articulated as follows: "free (as in speech), not free (as in beer)."

technically savvy users rather than everyday users that are not technically able to enjoy the rights that free software embodies.

The goals embodied by free software were codified in the "Four Freedoms" that Richard Stallman proposed and the Free Software Foundation published as a definition of free software in 1986. Those freedoms, with introductory explanation, are as follows:

Free software is a matter of the users' freedom to run, copy, distribute, study, change and improve the software. More precisely, it refers to four kinds of freedom, for the users of the software:

- The freedom to run the program, for any purpose (freedom 0).
- The freedom to study how the program works, and adapt it to your needs (freedom 1). Access to the source code is a precondition for this.
- The freedom to redistribute copies so you can help your neighbour (freedom 2).
- The freedom to improve the program, and release your improvements to the public, so that the whole community benefits (freedom 3). Access to the source code is a precondition for this.[6]

The purpose of these rules is novel: in terms of more traditional works of authorship, it would be as if an author of a short story wished to allow any reader to rework her story and

---

[6] The application of this definition in practice can be quite complex, as indicated by the supplemental notes that accompany the free software definition at the Free Software Foundation Web site, which can be found here: http://www.gnu.org/philosophy/free-sw.html

then share it with others — or even sell it — provided that those she sold it to were permitted the rights to do exactly the same thing. In short, the definition first specifies a' very broad set of freedoms, but then imposes a set of restrictions on the recipient of those freedoms, in order to ensure their extension to others.

The utilisation of this definition was intended to create a sort of public commons of software. That goal has been impressively achieved, in part because unlike many types of historically shared property, free software is protected by licenses that prevent the public engaging in the type of behaviour that too often results in the "tragedy of the commons" (that is, a tendency among those entitled to share in the commons to overexploit it for their own advantage until the resource is exhausted, before someone else does). A free software license is therefore self consciously both a social contract as well as a set of legal rules.[7]

Open Source Software

Open source software[8] embraces most of the same objectives as free software, but emphasises its attributes in a somewhat different fashion. Like the Free Software Foundation, there is a

---

[7] The novelty of the goals propounded by Stallman are reflected in the name he gave to the license intended to secure his four freedoms, which he named a "copyleft" license. The most prominent copyleft license is the GNU General Public License (GPL), utilized by Stallman's GNU project, and thousands of other software development projects around the world, including the Linux kernel. Version 3 of the GNU Public License was released in 2007 after extensive input, discussion and debate.

[8] There are various nuances and variations in the terminology used to describe open software, including "free and open source software" (FOSS) and "free/libre open source software" (FLOSS).

non-profit organisation (in this case the Open Source Institute[9]) that controls the definition of open source software, and which also maintains a (near identical) list of licenses that OSI has approved as meeting its own definition. These licenses provide a wide range of rule sets from which a developer may choose when making software available.

Open Hardware

In a few cases, "open hardware" is also being created. Current examples include semiconductor designs (Sun's SPARC architecture and the Power.org architecture)[10] and even mobile telephone handsets (OpenMoko is creating a line of fully open source mobile phones, based upon both a mobile Linux operating system as well as handsets of its own design).[11]

---

[9] OSI was founded in 1998 by Bruce Perens and Eric S. Raymond, in part in an effort to make the concept of open source software less threatening to the commercial marketplace. The current, lengthy list of licenses (many rarely used) that have been submitted and approved by OSI may be found here: http://opensource.org/licenses/alphabetical

[10] Sun open sourced the SPARC architecture in March of 2006. Interested engineers can participate in the further evolution of the architecture through the OpenSPARC Initiative, which maintains a Web site here: http://www.opensparc.net/ Power.org was established by IBM and supporting companies in 2004 to develop open standards, guidelines, best practices and certifications to support IBM's Power Architecture. Its Web site is here: http://www.power.org/home

[11] OpenMoko was announced by First International Computer (FIC) in 2006. Its Web site can be found at: http://www.openmoko.com/

Open Development

Just as vendors realised long ago that open standards could help create larger markets faster, platform vendors are now realising that making their platforms as open as possible can foster the development of a wide range of products and services by independent software vendors (ISVs) to the mutual benefit of all, and most particularly of the platform vendor itself. As a result, even traditionally closed and controlling vendors, such as telecommunications companies, are now competing to open up their (often Linux-based) mobile telephone operating systems in order to encourage ISVs to make the use of mobile phones more interesting and attractive. Already, several major vendor as well as community efforts have been launched, each with a different approach, and with a different member composition:[12]

LiMo (for Linux Mobile) Foundation, formed in January 2007 primarily by handset vendors. LiMo was founded to "create an open, Linux-based software platform for use by the whole global industry to produce mobile devices...enabling a rich ecosystem of

---

[12] On March 6, 2008, Apple's Steve Jobs announced his own, more limited and controlled effort at attracting ISVs to the iPhone platform. Under the Apple plan, ISVs can gain access to the necessary technical information to create applications to run on the iPhone, which Apple will then market through a new ""App Store" that it will host. I have doubts whether this more controlling effort will be as successful as the other, more open mobile efforts, as I discussed in a March 7, 2008 blog entry at The Standards Blog titled Steve Jobs Endangered Second Act, at http://www.consortiuminfo.org/standardsblog/article.php?story=20080307054430261&

differentiated products, applications, and services from device manufacturers, operators, ISVs and integrators."[13]

Open Handset Alliance,[14] announced on November 5, 2007. OHA is spearheaded by Google, and was supported by 33 additional members at launch, including mobile handset makers, application developers, some mobile carriers and chip makers. Like LiMo, OHA is developing a Linux-based open mobile platform, in this case called Android.

Moblin.org,[15] the Mobile and Internet Linux project, launched by Intel in July of 2007 as an open source project. Moblin is focused more broadly than LiMo and OHA, focusing on "mobile Internet devices," a more heterogeneous category than simply handsets. Canonical, the developer of the Ubuntu Linux distribution, is working on an operating system in support of the project.

GNOME Mobile & Embedded Initiative,[16] announced in April of 2007, and focused on the GNOME Linux-based operating system

---

[13] "Welcome to LiMo," at: http://www.limofoundation.org/welcome-to-limo.html accessed May 28, 2008.

[14] The home page for the Open Handset Alliance can be found here: http://www.openhandsetalliance.com/

[15] The Moblin.org Web site can be found at: http://www.moblin.org/

[16] The Gnome Mobile Web site can be found at: http://www.gnome.org/mobile/

Open Standards

The definition of open standards is at once the oldest as well as the (currently) most disputed. In traditional standard setting circles, "openness" was achieved through a rule set that sought to ensure that all "stakeholders" (i.e., not only those that implement standards, but also governments and those affected by standards as well) had access to the process, that consensus would drive decisions, that an appeals process would be provided, and that the IPR of a single stakeholder would not unreasonably stand in the way of the common good whenever that result could be achieved.

With the rise of the information and communications technology, however, this rule set began to become more constraining, for a variety of reasons, and particularly so in the case of software. Those reasons include the proliferation of patent "thickets," the convergence of technologies in single devices (such that a mobile telephone, for example, may infringe upon hundreds of patents as a result of complying with necessary standards), and the increasing deployment of open source software under licenses with terms that may not be satisfied when standards are implemented that were developed under traditional IPR policies.

The result has been an ongoing debate over the definition of what should constitute an "open standard," and particularly over what the IPR terms of the policies should be under which such standards are developed.[17]

---

[17] One of the most cited discussions of open standards attributes is Open Standards Requirements, by Ken Krechmer, at http://www.csrstds.com/openstds.pdf The International Journal of IT Standards and Standardization Research, Vol. 4 No. 1, January – June 2006. Krechmer's lists of attributes is sufficiently comprehensive, however, that very few standards organizations would likely to satisfy it.

Open content: The concept of open content is in many ways similar to open source and free software, but made generic to serve any type of copyrightable work, whether it be text, graphic, audio or video. As with software, a set of legal terms serving this concept has been proposed and become widely adopted as a result of the efforts of articulate visionaries that have (once again) created a non-profit entity to serve that vision. The most prominent advocate in this case is Stanford Law School professor Lawrence Lessig, and the resulting institution is called the Creative Commons.[18]

The goal of the Creative Commons is to encourage wider reuse of copyrightable works by providing easy to use, free legal tools that creators can use to provide such rights, for such purposes, and to such types of users, as they wish. This is accomplished through a series of plain language licenses (now translated into 43 languages) that make it easy for creators to make their work as freely and easily available as they wish. As explained at the Creative Commons Web site:

In the words of Thomas Jefferson, "He who receives an idea from me, receives instruction himself without lessening mine; as he who lights his taper at mine receives light without darkening me." An idea is not diminished when more people use it. Creative Commons aspires to cultivate a commons in which people can feel free to reuse not only ideas, but also words, images, and music without asking permission — because permission has already been granted to everyone.[19]

---

[18] The Creative Commons Web site can be found at: http://creativecommons.org/

[19] Excerpted from "Legal Concepts," Creative Commons, accessed May 18, 2008, at http://wiki.creativecommons.org/Legal_Concepts

We use private rights to create public goods: creative works set free for certain uses. Like the free software and open-source movements, our ends are cooperative and community-minded, but our means are voluntary and libertarian. We work to offer creators a best-of-both-worlds way to protect their works while encouraging certain uses of them — to declare "some rights reserved."[20]

The licenses themselves are visually coded to symbolically indicate the significant terms that each contains, making it easy for anyone to select the licensing approach most to their liking. The terms and their associated symbols are as follows:[21]

	Attribution. You let others copy, distribute, display, and perform your copyrighted work — and derivative works based upon it — but only if they give credit the way you request.
	Noncommercial. You let others copy, distribute, display, and perform your work — and derivative works based upon it — but for noncommercial purposes only.
	No Derivative Works. You let others copy, distribute, display, and perform only verbatim copies of your work, not derivative works based upon it.

---

[20] Excerpted from "About," Creative Commons, accessed May 18, 2008, at http://wiki.creativecommons.org/Legal_Concepts

[21] Excerpted from "License Your Work," Creative Commons, accessed May 18, 2008, at http://creativecommons.org/about/license/

Share Alike. You allow others to distribute derivative works only under a license identical to the license that governs your work.

Because the Creative Commons has created and maintains the source documentation for the licenses in three forms — plain language, legal "fine print," and machine-readable code that can be detected by search engines — a creator can place her work under the Creative Commons license of her choice in a matter of minutes.

The licenses provided by the Creative Commons have been very widely adopted, not only with respect to specific works, but also to all of the material at individual blogs, in photo collections at sites such as Flickr, and in many other situations on the Web. As a result, the Creative Commons has helped facilitate not only the reuse of much of the most easily available content, but also the workings of collaborative projects. Other projects, such as the Wikipedia, utilise the GNU Free Documentation License, which was created for a similar purpose.[22]

Open Data

The concept of open data is intended to encourage and enable broad availability of non-textual data of various, usually scientific types (e.g., genomic and mapping data). Due to the high economic value of much data of this type, and the fact that scientific data tends to be created in non-profit institutions and for-profit labs that are in each case subject to ownership policies

---

[22] The text of this license may be found at the GNU Project Web site at http://www.gnu.org/copyleft/fdl.html (accessed May 18, 2008). There are a number of other, less widely used open content licenses.

relating to IPR, the articulation and adoption of open data is thus far less advanced. However, the value of making data rapidly and widely available on the Internet in formats allowing it to be rapidly searched and integrated is obvious.

Open Access

Open access is a practice that relates to both open data and open content. The term was coined at a meeting held in Budapest in December of 2001 that led to the issuance of a call to action referred to as the Budapest Open Access Initiative.[23] Those that drafted the Initiative document recognised that there was great opportunity to be gained by returning to the historical practice of freely sharing scientific data and learning, so that the academic and scientific communities at large could benefit from, and build upon those contributions. In order to achieve those goals, the Initiative recommended both self publishing by researchers and authors (which it called Self-Archiving)[24] as well as the conversion of journals to on-line, searchable resources (which it referred to as Open Access Journals).

This call to action was met with enthusiasm. As of this writing, the Directory of Open Access Journals lists 1151 journals

---

[23] The text of the Initiative can be found at http://www.soros.org/openaccess/read.shtml (accessed May 18, 2008).

[24] Self-Archiving has been facilitated by the formation of the Open Archives Initiative, which develops standard for that purpose. The home page of this organization can be found at: http://www.openarchives.org/ (accessed May 18, 2008).

searchable at the article level, exposing a total of 184,817 articles in all to search engines and direct searches.[25]

Lessons Learned and Next Steps

As can be appreciated from the high level overview of open methodologies offered above, the very brief existence of the Internet and the Web has led to broad appreciation of the benefits that can arise from greater visibility and collaboration. The examples given also demonstrate a great deal of creativity in using traditional legal tools in an effort to facilitate and encourage such activity. In each case, these tools have been created to address a desire to rebalance the traditional rights of creators and inventors with those that wish to build upon their efforts.

It is important to note that while this willingness to share is to some extent based upon moral or ethical grounds, it is also firmly rooted in self interest. In every case noted above, those that are willing to give more also anticipate getting more, with this new potential made possible by the global reach of the Internet and the searchable nature of the Web. In consequence, it would appear that the trend towards openness is likely to be fundamental and sustaining, rather than a passing fad.

It is important to recognise the magnitude of this revolution, because it indicates that another fundamental shift — this time in law, or at least in legal tools — is both warranted as well as desirable, in order to capitalise on the benefits that increased sharing can offer. To date, these benefits have sometimes been trivialised, with proponents of legal change pointing only to (for example) pop cultural "mashups" of audio and video clips on

---

[25] The index of the Directory of Open Access Journals can be found at http://www.doaj.org/ (accessed May 18, 2008).

YouTube. While such activities are certainly not trivial to those involved in the arts, they do not represent the examples most likely to head off the legions of lobbyists that could be expected to descend upon legislators if changes were feared that would apply equally to semiconductor chip designs, the text of best selling novels and the formulations of blockbuster pharmaceuticals.

What Can Be Gained

Changes of any nature to existing laws will require strong justifications. It is therefore useful to summarise some of the ways that a liberalisation of laws and practices can benefit society, as well as provide off-setting benefits to IPR owners as well. Consider, for example, the benefits that can accrue from the following:

- More rapid development of projects of all types, due to the ability of more like-minded individuals to join in collaborative communities than before, and from greater freedom to reuse and incorporate the work of others

- More rapid scientific discoveries, because information can be accessed and searched immediately upon disclosure on line, and then used as the basis for further discoveries

- Greater opportunities for those in emerging societies, as a result of a more level playing in research and development, through free and unrestricted access to more data, software and open content

- Greater ease of entry for new businesses in developed societies, resulting from lower barriers to entry through use of open technologies, data, content and other material

- Reduced prices and greater profits, as a result of widely shared development costs

Many of these benefits are already being realised. But some impediments remain, chiefly in the area of patents, but also under copyright law.

What May Need To Change

As already demonstrated by the development and widespread use of FOSS, open source and Creative Commons licenses, a great deal of creativity has already been invested in adapting old tools to serve new uses. But there are limits to how far this process can be taken. The following are examples of areas in which legislative action, organic evolution through the courts, or additional non-profit organisations might be useful:

Fair Use

Traditional fair use doctrines have permitted only extremely limited reuses of copyright material. Currently, only a few words can be safely reused in most situations, and not a great deal more even where (as in literary reviews) more extensive excerpts can be incorporated. At the same time, the degree of tolerance for reuse in the breach is changing, in some cases dramatically, as content owners often reap indirect financial rewards as a result of such borrowing. Examples of such practices include news links at blogs that include news article outtakes that often exceed fair use length, but then provide a link back to the content owner's site, thereby driving traffic and enhancing revenues. In some cases, such reuse is even desired and encouraged as part of modern marketing campaigns.

Software Patents

The current state of U.S. patent law as it relates to software seems to please just about no one, although there is a wide variety of opinion on how the law and the operations of the United States Patent and Trademark Office (PTO) should change. Leaving aside calls to abolish patent protection for software entirely, there is consensus that patents are too easy to get, and too hard and expensive to challenge when they have been improperly granted. Any progress in cutting down on the density of so-called "patent thickets" would provide at least some incremental relief.

Increased Use Of Non-assertion Covenants

A commitment made by a patent owner that it would not assert its "essential claims" against compliant implementations of a given standard has been a permissible alternative to agreeing to providing an implementation licenses on RAND terms in some standards organisations for many years. More recently, such pledges have been made in connection with FOSS and open source software as well. In principle, such promises are much better than a commitment to license, since no action on the part of the beneficiary of the pledge is required at all, and because it is apparent to all that everyone benefits to exactly the same degree (as compared to the licensing situation, where specific terms are usually known only to the parties on a license by license basis).

But pledges, like license commitments, do have some limitations, such as variations in terms, and difficulty of enforcement against later owners of the patents in question. These weaknesses could be solved, in the first instance, by an organisation that maintained a list of pledges that had been found to meet minimum standards for FOSS licensing, and in the second instance, by setting up a registry with the PTO that would allow a patent to be permanently encumbered with the obligation assumed, much as a mortgage filed with a registry of deeds enables an enforceable obligation to be imposed on a successor owner of real property.

Summary

During the years of the Internet Bubble, it was fashionable to observe that the Internet had "changed everything." That observation seemed naïve and without basis by 2001. But with time it has become apparent that the Internet really has changed some things in a fundamental and permanent way. One of those things is the way in which knowledge can be created and shared.

There is ample evidence that this more limited observation is sound, and that much can be gained by taking appropriate action to encourage and facilitate the ways in which the Internet can be utilised for the purpose of sharing information as widely and quickly as possible, and collaboratively building upon that information in as unrestricted a fashion as possible.

This process is already well along, through the organic efforts of a wide variety of both visionaries as well as lesser mortals, who together are creating and promoting new tools that have already enjoyed wide and successful adoption. This grass roots process will no doubt continue, and may in fact be best suited to realising the potential of a wired world for some time to come.

While this experimental process continues, restraint on the part of legislatures, and a willingness to be open minded on the part of the courts, may provide the best route to eventually settling on a new balance between the IPR rights of creators and inventors, on the one hand, and re-users and end-users on the other.

When that process is complete, the more traditional process of law making and treaty drafting can step in to memorialise and formalise the solutions worked out in the trenches, based on the wisdom gained through the rough and tumble of the marketplace.

Andrew Updegrove is a co-founder and partner of the Boston law firm of Gesmer Updegrove LLP. Since 1988 he has served as legal counsel to over 135 standards development organizations and open source foundations, most of which he has helped structure and launch. He has been retained by many of the largest technology companies in the world to assist them in forming such organizations.

He has also written and spoken extensively on the topics of consortia, standard setting and open source software, has given testimony to the United States Department of Justice, Federal Trade Commission, and Congressional and State legislative committees on the same topics, and has filed "friend of the court" briefs on a pro bono basis with the Federal Circuit Court, Supreme Court, and Federal Trade Commission in support of standards development in leading standards-related litigation. In 2002, he launched ConsortiumInfo.org, a website intended to be the most detailed and comprehensive resource on the Internet on the topics of consortia and standard setting, as well as Standards Today, a bi-monthly eJournal of news, ideas and analysis in the standard setting and open source areas with over 7,000 subscribers around the world. In 2005, he launched the Standards Blog. ConsortiumInfo.org serves over 10 million page views annually.

He has been a member of the United States Standards Strategy revision committee, and received the President's Award for Journalism from American National Standards Institute (ANSI) in 2005. His current and past Board service includes the Boards of Directors of ANSI, the Linux Foundation and the Free Standards Group, and the Boards of Advisors of HL7 and Open Source for America. He is a graduate of Yale University and the Cornell University Law School.

Open Innovation in the Real World

By Shane Coughlan

"Open innovation is a paradigm that assumes that firms can and should use external ideas as well as internal ideas, and internal and external paths to market, as the firms look to advance their technology"
Professor Henry Chesbrough

Open Innovation is one of the most frequently cited terms in Information Technology. It is applied to software, to data, and to hardware. It manifests itself in practically all discussions around standards and access to information. Whenever an argument can be made for increased collaboration or sharing, Open Innovation is invariably proposed as an approach that offers an equitable solution for the majority of stakeholders involved. But what is it, and how does it work in the real world?

A quick visit to Wikipedia suggests that Open Innovation was invented by Professor Chesbrough and is essentially about reducing the cost of research and development. This is accomplished by looking outside of the closed world of a single company from an Intellectual Property perspective, and buying or licensing third-party innovation to get a competitive advantage. Under this reading it offers the potential for improved productivity, it allows the inclusion of customers early in the development process, increased accuracy in targeting and better marketing. Procter & Gamble's "Connect and Develop" (C&D) is cited as a success for this form of Open Innovation, allowing the company to improve research productivity through global collaboration.

In this context Open Innovation is the opposite of what can be termed Closed Innovation, which advocates the strict control and ownership of Intellectual Property. The underlying concept of Closed Innovation is that a company can benefit from having complete control of the new product development cycle, and it assumes that one party can obtain the necessary economic resources to accomplish this goal. Closed Innovation, though only explicitly named after Open Innovation gained traction as a concept, was the dominant form of innovation observed in the 20th century. It explicitly address what are identified as potential disadvantages in Open Innovation. Namely, revealing information not intended for sharing, the loss of competitive advantage due to such revelations, and increased complexity to control innovation due the requirement to engage with third parties.

While neat, this reading of Open Innovation and Closed Innovation as opposite Intellectual Property management techniques is somewhat limited, and hardly describes the wealth of "openness" we are observing today in technology, art and manufacturing. This paper proposes that there is value in observing the broader picture rather than myopically focusing on IPR strategy. It therefore contextualises Open Innovation as an umbrella term for approaches to openness in individual fields. The unifying concept is to share ideas in a way that helps stakeholders obtain useful solutions today and a fertile ground for developing solutions tomorrow. It accomplishes this by providing a method to bring many minds to bear in the consideration of issues. From this perspective the roots of Open Innovation lie more with the Greek schools of philosophy than with business courses. It can be understood as emerging during the Middle Ages, when scientific method became common, and peer review or the discussion of results became the norm in advancing knowledge.

"The best way to have a good idea is to have a lot of ideas."
Dr. Linus Pauling

With the advent of computers and the Internet, sharing ideas became easier due to decreases in relative distance between and increases in absolute scale around common interest groups. This was especially observable in the area of computer science itself. Programmers often asserted that they could make better code by sharing algorithms with other developers to check for errors and refine the mathematics. Over the past thirty years this process of sharing was formalised into what are commonly called the rules of "Free Software." The underlying concept is that everyone collaborating on a problem agrees to provide the ability to use, study, share and improve the applicable code, and this results in increased potential value for all parties concerned. In recent times this concept has been marketed as a development approach to companies under the name "Open Source."

The precise value delivered by open collaborative approaches has yet to be fully defined, though some of the numbers currently in circulation make it clear that Open Source is a powerful economic driver. Research from Gartner and IDC shows that Open Source is present in up to 90% of commercial code and that it directly underwrites a 50 billion USD economy based on collaboration. It powers phones, TVs and appliances across the world, and is rapidly entering areas like automation and automotive production. But these hard numbers and facts may not be the most interesting aspect of Open Innovation. The simple rules of Free Software that allow for programmers to use, study, share and improve software have been gradually expanded and reapplied to many other fields.

We can find Open Innovation applied to books, pictures, and music through the umbrella of the Creative Commons. This is a massive wealth of creative works that offer more flexibility and international applicability than Public Domain while maintaining a low barrier to entry for new participants. We can also find Open Innovation applied to raw information through projects like Wikipedia and OpenStreetMap. These act as global showcases for how broad participation can profoundly impact our ability to access local and global knowledge. We even see Open Innovation in hardware, a field not normally considered to fall within the remit of creative works. There are now Open Hardware printers, computer processors, cars and robots. Today Open Innovation allows everyone to share virtually anything with anyone else, anywhere in the world.

"The world is but a canvas to our imaginations."
Henry David Thoreau

Allowing people to use, study, share and improve creative works provides value for the stakeholders involved. This implies a "network effect" of collaboration, based on the underlying understanding that no company can employ all the minds that can potentially contribute to solving a problem. Indeed, no single entity can bring more than a fraction of the potential minds to bear. Collaboration addresses this by tapping into a much broader pool. In theory at least it leads to better, quicker and more effective solutions. The proviso is that broad collaboration needs to be kept simple and it needs to be kept fair to operate, and it needs to do so in the context of complex markets. This introduces two substantial challenges to realising effective solutions.

The first is that different stakeholders will have different motivations for participation, especially when some originate from different industries, countries or cultures. Everyone needs to agree on the same rules or the value of participation will be undermined for all parties concerned. Yet the larger the group gathered to address a challenge, the greater the chance that someone will not understand or support all of those rules. The second is that the collaborative stakeholders are only one part of a puzzle. No matter how broad the collaboration observed in a market segment, it will never be uniform. Third parties - who may be completely uninterested in collaboration with the aforementioned stakeholders - can also have a profound impact on the collaborative endeavour in question. Therefore collaboration will inherently be subject to disruption from disinterested (or openly hostile) third parties.

The first situation can be illustrated by considering a single supply chain where companies are competing to develop components, companies are competing to build products, and companies are competing to put their badge on products and sell them. In areas like software or consumer electronics, the companies may have a development as well as purchasing relationships, and therefore collectively contribute to certain shared platforms that enable the deployed products. Each collaborative stakeholder has subtly different motivations for participation. If a single company tries to gain an advantage by bending the rules around collaborative development, then all the other companies will have a good reason to rethink future sharing.

The second situation can be illustrated by considering a market area which contains both collaborative stakeholders and third parties who can impact interaction but have no investment in its continuation. For example, if some companies choose to collaborate on software to reduce Research and Development costs, there is a motivation for a third party to interrupt or halt that collaboration as a competitive measure. The intervention may be the form of enticing individual companies into rival initiatives or it may be in the form of aggressive intervention through patent litigation or similar measures. Regardless, causing collaborators to dissolve or reduce their interaction will provide relief to a competitor, and is therefore ample motivation for such actions. Of course, it also introduces the question of whether the actions are motivated by true competitiveness or attempting to obtain a form of market stasis, but that is largely a discussion for another time.

> *"There is nothing more difficult to take in hand, more perilous to conduct, or more uncertain in its success, than to take the lead in the introduction of a new order of things."*
> Niccolo Machiavelli

Open Innovation has a long history, a high rate of adoption, and is accompanied by compelling economic figures. It clearly offers a lot of potential to solve important challenges in the context of increased globalisation and competitiveness, particularly with regards to advancing research and the application of existing solutions to new areas. However, it is also somewhat fragile, and depends on a certain amount of goodwill between stakeholders, a certain degree of fairness in markets, and a certain amount of recourse for injured parties when either goodwill or fairness is found to be lacking. While critics may object at this point and suggest that special exceptions cannot be made for one approach to technology or creativity, it can equally be proposed that a certain expectation of goodwill and market fairness is a long-established precedent in the use of Intellectual Property.   The real question is really whether the existing measures, largely born of a time when what is now termed Closed

Innovation was dominant, are still equitable in the context of the expanded marketplace we see today.

The adoption of Open Innovation by so many parties is not based on potential alone, but rather is informed by a series of social, economic and creative imperatives. In this context the discourse naturally transfers away from innovation per se, and instead towards the observable evolution of markets facing increased complexity, competition, and commodification. In such a situation, the value added by each individual company and each individual product is inherently smaller and less exclusive than in simpler economic times, but simultaneously the pooling of knowledge and the development of common platforms allows for sophisticated solutions to be introduced faster than before. The question is how do modern societies address the challenge of ensuring that Open and Closed approaches to innovation are allowed free, fair and complete competition in this context. Answering this question is the challenge of this coming decade, and it inevitably means that our understandings of "openness", "innovation", "competition" and "fairness" will be challenged, redefined, and reapplied. So they should be.

> *"The greatest danger in times of turbulence is not the turbulence; it is to act with yesterdays logic."*
> Peter Drucker

Shane Coughlan is an expert in communication methods and business development. He is best known for building bridges between commercial and non-commercial stakeholders in the technology sector. His professional accomplishments include establishing a legal department for the main NGO promoting Free Software in Europe, building a professional network of over 270 legal counsel and technical experts across 4 continents, and aligning corporate and community interests to launch the first law review dedicated to Free/Open Source Software.

Shane has extensive knowledge of Internet technologies, management best practice, community building and Free/Open Source Software. His experience includes engagement with the server, desktop, embedded and mobile telecommunication industries. He does business in Europe, Asia and the Americas, and maintains a broad network of contacts.

Examples

Bottom-Up Creation of
Open Scientific Knowledge

By Peter Murray-Rust et al

When OpenForum Academy sent out a call for its second book, we felt the need to contribute a piece on the enormous upwelling of openness in the scientific process. At the Open Knowledge Foundation, we had already published a chapter in the last book and felt this was a good opportunity to present some of our ideas and culture to a readership who would appreciate it.

'Open Science' is too big and multifaceted a term to be defined precisely. It covers at least the spectrum of materials, process, culture, formal specifications and activities. At the Open Knowledge Foundation (OKFN), we have many people interested in Open Science and have a dedicated working group (http://science.okfn.org/), blogs (http://science.okfn.org/blog/all-blog-posts/) and mailing list (http://lists.okfn.org/mailman/listinfo/open-science).

Rather than try to summarise it, we brought together stories under the umbrella of 'bottom-up Open Science'. Several people volunteered and we have included everyone who contributed. We have discussed how free and open source software can make a difference in science making through the enlightening example of the Blue Obelisk, have approached the 'Quantified Self' movement, have addressed libraries as more than ever needed tool for knowledge discovery and organisation, and have summed up the whole through the lenses of 'citizen science' thus proposing a new common denominator for open knowledge.

These stories are very varied but all have the core belief that individuals and small groups, working together, can make a difference by changing ideas, setting up tools and content and -- most importantly -- by growing communities.

Bottom-up Open Chemistry – the Blue Obelisk

Chemical software and data is a major activity, almost certainly exceeding 1 billion USD per year. However, almost all of it is closed, represented mainly by domain-specific software companies and traditional STM publishers. This is often aggressively protected; when the NIH set up an Open[*] database of chemicals and compounds the American Chemical Society (ACS) lobbied politically to have this curtailed and threatened Wikipedia with legal action for publishing the widely used CAS identifiers for chemicals. A major software producer will take legal action against licensees who publish program output, including bugs.

A number of independent, often unfunded, chemical hacker activities grew up during the 1990's and by 2000 a handful of codes were available but there was little continuity or coordination. We used to meet occasionally at ACS meetings and in 2006 we met in a bar near the large Blue Obelisk in Horton Plaza , San Diego. We felt that we had a consensus of philosophy, that the world undervalued our software and that we had the potential to change the future. We then agreed to loosely coordinate (not pool) our efforts. I suggested the name "Blue Obelisk" and our mantra ODOSOS – "Open data, Open Standards, Open Source ". To support this we created a Wiki, a mailing list and agreed to meet for dinner whenever we had a critical mass. There is no budget, no membership, no formal mechanisms – the mantra is our collective and very powerful DNA.

This has proved extremely successful and might work in other disciplines. We have about twenty projects which are happy to be counted as Blue Obelisk (http://en.wikipedia.org/wiki/Blue_Obelisk) and which fit into our criteria of ODOSOS. Our dinners are open to all – and closed source providers have attended and been relaxed. In 2007 we published a paper outlining our components. Recently we reviewed this in a 2011 paper with about 20 groups as authors.

When someone or organisation does something meritorious (normally an identifiable software product or data resource) I award a quartz Blue Obelisk (remarkably these are common and inexpensive). These loose traditions work. We now have software components in most of the chemical infrastructure for pharmaceuticals and increasingly in materials. The biggest problem is data – chemists do not publish machine computable data (though they should), instead embedding a subset in formal, subscription-access publications. We have machine extraction software but risk being prosecuted for extracting data.

Governance is minimal and we have been blessedly spared from either factionalism or imperialism. Each project is self-contained but uses other Blue Obelisk libraries where possible or more recently runs them as web services. The main language is Java, followed by Python and C(++) – with some historical FORTRAN. There is generally a leader to each project and while the Benevolent Dictator for Life (BDFL) occurs the commonest is "Doctor Who", where the Doctor hands on to a successor at irregular intervals.

Originally dismissed as cranks, we are now taken seriously. Companies such as Kitware, NY and Chemical Computing Group contribute significant amounts of code and as importantly, the critical mass of internal and external confidence. National labs (e.g. Pacific Northwest National Laboratory in US) have been awarded a Blue Obelisk for collaborating on Open Source. We know that our code is widely used in pharmaceutical companies but we have few metrics on this usage, which is a common problem of Open Source in secretive industries.

As with all volunteer Open Source projects we do not have clear timelines, but progress over the last 5 years has been very good. It's possible to find high-quality components in most subdomains, including unit and regression testing.

The main problems we face are that chemistry (surprisingly) often does not engineer its own solutions but prefers to buy them. This puts a value on shrink-wrapping and hand-held maintenance which gratis Open Source cannot easily provide. Academics producing new code often get little credit and it's worse when they re-engineer existing solutions, even when the result is markedly superior. It's also difficult to get funding ("it's a solved problem"). The fragmented nature of the commercial domain makes semantic interoperability very difficult –companies protect legacy walled garden approaches. The internal messes created by unvalidated variants of legacy files in the pharma industry (e.g. when the result of a merger requires data reconciliation) has probably cost well over 100 million dollars in human effort, while the Blue Obelisk could have provided common semantics.

However I think we are approaching a breakthrough. Chemical software has made few objective advances in the last 10-15 years such that we have now implemented most of the major algorithms as Open Source. For an organisation which takes a responsible view of costs and values innovation, the Blue Obelisk can be an attractive part of a solution.

Sample Size of One
By Bastian Grashake

The Quantified Self (QS) movement is a community of people who perform bottom-up citizen science every day. Many participants of the QS community meticulously collect different kinds of data about themselves: dietary composition, calorie intake, physical exercises, sleep habits, even dreams. More recently, metabolites, genetic variations and the composition of their bacterial communities – metagenomes - have become the subject of their self-surveillance. Such strict monitoring may seem strange and too cumbersome to be performed outside the realms of professional top athletes. However, recent technological advances such as the emergence of wearable consumer-oriented activity trackers (recording, for example, the number of steps the wearer has taken over time) and sleep trackers (monitoring the stages of sleep), combined with the rise of direct-to-consumer (DTC) genetic testing now offer easy ways to collect larger quantities of data about oneself.

It is not mere narcissism, but curiosity and desire to understand one's own body that drives involvement to the QS movement. Which workouts bring the effects I'm looking for? How does my diet not only influence my weight but maybe also my mood? Which drugs work best or have the least side-effects? And such data may also be used to ask more obscure questions: What effect has a shared bed on my sleep quality?[26] How does my butter intake influence my math-skills?[27]

---

[26] http://gedankenstuecke.github.com/blog/2012/09/26/on-getting-sleep/

[27] http://quantifiedself.com/2011/12/butter-and-arithmetic-how-much-butter/

QS participants thus use their data to perform experiments. By design, these are done unblinded and their sample size of one is as small as possible. These features may appear as an obstacle. These experiments, however, are performed by people who deeply care about the questions on hand. While most of these experiments probably will never enter the canon of peer-reviewed science, they are not doomed to fade away unnoticed. Many participants of the QS movement are out-going, and share their experiences and results. They write about their results in blogs such as QuantifiedSelf.com and meet for yearly conferences in the US and Europe.[28] Many cities worldwide now host monthly QS meetings where people share their practices and results by answering three questions: What did you do? How did you do it? What did you learn? This exchange – both online and offline – inspires community members to try similar approaches, to reproduce earlier results, or to modify experiments according to their needs.

Many people who are active in the QS movement are also openly sharing their data with others, thus allowing for experiments that overcome the limitations of the sample size of one. One of the most famous examples of this approach is the study on the effects of lithium carbonate in patients with amyotrophic lateral sclerosis (ALS), performed by users of the PatientsLikeMe community. In 2008, academic researchers published a study suggesting that regular intake of lithium carbonate could be used to slow down the progress of ALS, a currently incurable disease.[29] Following these observations, members of PatientsLikeMe started the off-label use of lithium

---

[28] http://quantifiedself.com/conference/Amsterdam-2013/

[29] http://www.pnas.org/content/105/6/2052.long

carbonate aiming to slow down their ALS. By comparing the disease progression of users who did and did not take lithium carbonate, the PatientsLikeMe data showed that the drug is not effective in slowing down the disease.[30]

Thus, a highly motivated group of patients using the Internet allowed a clinical study to be performed at a low cost and largely outside of academia. Following this success, similar projects have burgeoned: Genomera,[31] a San Francisco-based start-up, offers a community dedicated to the idea of small-scale studies. Users can create new studies, give input on the experimental design and enrol as participants. The non-commercial openSNP project[32][33] is similarly interested in genetics. Users can upload their genetic data along with further physiological details about themselves. For example, daily step counts or weight as collected by QS sensors can be provided, as can information about hair colour and diseases using text fields and images. The goal is to create an open database (the data being released under a Creative Commons Zero waiver) that can be used for studies seeking new associations of genetic variations with diseases and traits.

From people collecting seemingly unimportant data to real studies with medical significance: many participants of the QS movement are already performing science. They share results and data, replicate earlier findings and organise conferences. Most of this is done outside of academia, unfunded and without any central organisation. The collaborations of those highly motivated

---

[30] http://www.nature.com/nbt/journal/v29/n5/full/nbt.1837.html

[31] http://genomera.com/OLIJHOEK

[32] https://opensnp.org

[33] Disclosure: Bastian Greshake is a developer of openSNP.

science amateurs show how science can be performed in a bottom-up fashion and how they can complement research performed in academia and industry. With more and more people joining the QS movement, with new ways of sharing data, knowledge and insights won through self-tracking, and by collaborating the impact of their efforts will rise in the future.

A new role for libraries in open access information management
By Tom Olihjoek

The dissemination of knowledge on a large scale only became possible through the distribution of books and journals by publishers among a growing group of (highly) educated people. Prior to the introduction of the Internet in the 1990s, publishers had built up a monopoly on the production and distribution of knowledge through printed scientific journals and books. Publishers were justifying the ever increasing costs of subscriptions to scientific journals by the increased production and distribution costs. Scientists and research institutions had no choice but to pay.

After the Internet became popular, modern digital reproduction and distribution made these costs almost negligible. The publishers, however, have continued to increase their prices and to shield most publications from free access online. Consequently, scientists, institutes and other knowledge seekers still pay large sums to publishers for a now basically redundant service. Moreover, these developments have forced libraries to drastically cut-back on their subscriptions to scientific journals. The role of libraries is seemingly also undermined by an increasing number of scientists who read and publish work in open access journals, which can be accessed without library subscriptions. Libraries thus suffer from an 'identity crisis' as they are forced to re-assess their role as suppliers of information.

Noticeably, the past few years have shown a spectacular growth of the number of open access publications. As of April 2013, the Directory of Open Access Journals[34] lists over 8,000 journals publishing articles under the terms of permissive Creative Commons licenses. While the volume of information available online dramatically increases, the difficulty of finding relevant information in the resulting haystack becomes more pressing every day.

This 'information glut' creates a growing need to find ways of making accumulated knowledge easily accessible. Just because open access information is accessible does not mean that specific information is easy to find, let alone that the reliability of the information can be easily determined. While access may no longer be an issue, discoverability is. By discoverability I mean that information should be easy to find and that access sites should be easy to use. The problem with the combined knowledge accumulated on the internet is that information of interest to specific communities is often too scattered and fragmented to be useful for them. Anybody in need of specific information has to dig, find and curate an ever increasing number of sources. All this leads to a general feeling that the information is out there but is "too big to know."[35] Some scientists claim this is not a problem as all information, even scattered all over the internet, will always be easily found with the appropriate indexing and computer search algorithms. In my view, we would be putting too much trust in computers. Even if computers would function flawlessly all the

---

[34] Directory of Open Access Journals (DOAJ) http://doaj.org

[35] David Weinberger (2012) Too big to Know http://amzn.to/11Du4Fd

time (and we know this not to be true), there is always the risk of only finding information that companies or government bodies want you to find. The search algorithms referred to as "personalised search services" are very much on the rise,[36] but wouldn't it be far better to organise information according to topics ourselves?

At first sight, the classical library function of offering access to information may appear to become of lesser importance in a 100% open access situation, but I see a new role emerging where libraries and librarians will start to organise open access content in a way that the public and scientists can use it best.[37][38] One way of doing this would be for libraries to take on the task of organising information around topics. Thus, libraries could reclaim their central role in making information accessible, a role which they have had all along but which has become much more complex after the invention of the internet and the digital revolution that followed. One such initiative has already started: the Open Library of Humanities wants to be a platform for open access publications in the field of humanities.[39]

There are many advantages of organising information by topics. For one, the discoverability of the information would improve, second communities interested in the topic could collaborate with libraries to keep information up to date and third

---

[36] Eli Pariser (2012) The filter bubble. http://amzn.to/11DtR4Y

[37] Bjoern Brembs Blog: open access taking off: Visions2: http://bjoern.brembs.net/comment-n894.html

[38] What role do university librarians play in access to research? http://bit.ly/14qeNVW

[39] Open Library of Humanities http://www.openlibhums.org/

community efforts could shape information in such a way that everyone can find information on his or her level of understanding.

Collaboration between scientists, libraries and communities could be a first step in the creation of an Open Science society, where most science is not kept hidden behind toll-access bars, but has an active role in sharing knowledge between all people on the planet.

The rebirth of the citizen scientist
By Rayna Stamboliyska

In the recent decade, the term 'citizen science' has emerged to define public involvement in genuine research projects. Synonym labels such as 'crowd-sourced science,'

or 'networked science' actually represent a new make-up for an old idea: back in 1982, science theoretician Feyerabend advocated the "democratisation of science." Going more decades backwards in time, Thomas Jefferson used to envision[40] weather stations operated by volunteers as a means for people to be informed and educated thus engaging into self-governance, a dynamics that is currently happening for real.[41]

This Jeffersonian idea illustrates one of the basic and most crucial issues with science as it is currently performed (i.e., through research within official institutions): its isolation. Contrastingly, citizen science operates – by design – free of the constraints inherent to such strongly formalised places. Citizen

---

[40] http://blogs.scientificamerican.com/guest-blog/2012/07/03/life-liberty-and-the-pursuit-of-data/

[41] http://wxqa.com/

science thus not only relocates science, but it also fosters its growth in the mainstream of society. Non-professionals join professionals, thus co- creating knowledge that makes science an integral part of our daily lives and shared human culture.

Numerous examples can be quoted, each bringing its unique colour and shape to the picturesque landscape of citizen science: from birdwatchers illustrating[42] how times of nesting shift as a consequence of climate change to disaster management,[43] from mapping roadkill accidents[44] to producing one's fluorescent yoghurt at home.[45] These projects illustrate a shift in public engagement in science: from citizens being solely data collectors to data analysts, visualisers and generators of new hypotheses. The hacker and DIY movements have widely contributed to the emergence of a true citizen science, i.e. one that fully explores human curiosity in a non-professional context.

Citizen science is in its infancy yet its popularity grows exponentially as the concept is modular enough to reach the humanities and social sciences (HSS),[46] generally overlooked by both professionals from the so-called "hard" sciences, and citizens. HSS are studies of human nature at large. They

---

[42] http://nestwatch.org/

[43] http://www.huffingtonpost.com/w-david-stephenson/citizen-science-disaster-information_b_1321899.html

[44] http://www.huffingtonpost.com/2012/05/11/adventurers-scientists-for-conservation_n_1510048.html

[45] http://www.indiebiotech.com/?p=152

[46] http://blogs.plos.org/citizensci/2013/02/25/science-and-society-voices-from-the-humanities-and-social-sciences/

encounter the same issues as the "hard" sciences: popularisation and communication, policy questions, and a wide range of ethical concerns. Additionally and similarly, HSS have particular theoretical traditions, methodological orientations, and critical interests.

The recent surge of citizen science, greatly assisted by information and communication technologies, thus allows reconsideration of the somewhat artificial categorisations of science domains and naturally involves trans- and interdisciplinary in scientific practise.

These considerations indicate that one does not need a ten-person lab, multimillion-dollar grants and caffeine-intoxicated PhDs in order to perform brilliant science. Citizen systems of participation aimed at collective problem-solving bring, however, two crucial questions: Is citizen science capable of producing reliable data? What guarantees do we have that it is ethical science?

Engaging huge numbers of citizens in a research project means that massive input is generated. Indeed, volunteers already collect data for scientific projects: how reliable is this? Two decades ago, the USA introduced an amendment prohibiting volunteer-collected data to be used in the US National Biological Survey. In the case of a community-based bird species diversity survey, the estimated number of birds correlated with the changes in numbers of observers. Such examples contribute to a stigma associated with citizen science data, which is sometimes labelled 'incompetent' or 'biased.' In a recent piece, John Gollan argues[47] the opposite: "a growing body of literature shows that data collected by citizens are comparable to those of professional scientists." Although data-integrity issues can occur, Gollan

---

[47] http://blog.okfn.org/2013/01/23/citizen-science-can-produce-reliable-data/

highlights an important message: "it's just a matter of honing in on those

particular issues and addressing them if necessary. This can be through training to improve skill sets or calibrating data where possible."

The second question that springs to mind when opening scientific practiceto non-professionals is ethics. Many have voiced concerns[48] about dubious ethical frameworks in various citizen science projects. The project that caused recent kerfuffle was uBiome, a project to sequence human genome entirely supported through crowd-funding. Indeed, research ethics are not something to play with: thus, every project dealing with human subjects requires the review and approval of an independent committee – generally referred to as Institutional Review Board (IRB) – prior to its start. The uBiome citizen science project was thoroughly criticised for seeking IRB review of their protocols only after the crowd-funding campaign was completed. A similarly strict review framework is de rigour when a research project involves animal subjects. In a recent piece for Scientific American,[49] professional scientist and citizen science advocate Caren Cooper called for community answers to ethical questions as the boundary between hobby practitioners and citizen scientists is too blurry to be defined, and so are the cases in which participants need to be invited to follow official ethics

---

[48]   http://boundarylayerphysiology.com/2013/02/17/why-im-worried-about-ethical-shenanigans-in-the-citizen-science-movement/

[49]   http://blogs.scientificamerican.com/guest-blog/2013/03/05/animal-care-ethics-in-citizen-science-my-conundrum/

protocols. As also exemplified by numerous reactions from open and citizen science enthusiasts,[50] IRB approval can be a hurdle for citizen scientists.

Cooper's call-out to the community of both professional and citizen scientists does echo a widely shared concern:[51] is there someone – and if so, who? – to provide oversight of DIYbio/ citizen science practices? By design, both professional and citizen scientists need to urgently address this particular and foundational issue.

None of us can continue standing passive when a threat is posed to citizen science. It fosters our common culture of curiosity and bridges gaps between people whose personal aims and leisure-time activities converge on a desire to advance research and improve human welfare and communities.

---

[50] http://storify.com/PatrikD/is-irb-approval-a-significant-hurdle-for-diybio-pu

[51] http://scio13.wikispaces.com/Session+6B

Peter Murray-Rust is a contemporary chemist born in Guildford in 1941. He was educated at Bootham School and Balliol College, Oxford. After obtaining a Doctor of Philosophy he became lecturer in chemistry at the (new) University of Stirling and was first warden of Andrew Stewart Hall of Residence. In 1982 he moved to Glaxo Group Research at Greenford to head Molecular Graphics, Computational Chemistry and later protein structure determination. He was Professor of Pharmacy in the University of Nottingham from 1996-2000, setting up the Virtual School of Molecular Sciences. He is now Reader in Molecular Informatics at the University of Cambridge and Senior Research Fellow of Churchill College.

His research interests have involved the automated analysis of data in scientific publications, creation of virtual communities e.g. The Virtual School of Natural Sciences in the Globewide Network Academy and the Semantic Web. With Henry Rzepa he has extended this to chemistry through the development of Markup languages, especially Chemical Markup Language. He campaigns for Open Data, particularly in science, and is on the advisory board of the Open Knowledge Foundation and a co-author of the Panton Principles for Open scientific data. Together with a few other chemists he was a founder member of the Blue Obelisk movement in 2005.

In 2002, Peter Murray-Rust and his colleagues proposed an electronic repository for unpublished chemical data called the World Wide Molecular Matrix (WWMM). In January 2011 a symposium around his career and visions was organized, called Visions of a Semantic Molecular Future. In 2011 he and Henry Rzepa were joint recipients of the Herman Skolnik Award of the American Chemical Society.

Bringing Geographic Data Into the Open with OpenStreetMap

By Coleman McCormick

With the growth of the open data movement, governments and data publishers are looking to enhance citizen participation. OpenStreetMap, the wiki of world maps, is an exemplary model for how to build community and engagement around map data. Lessons can be learned from the OSM model, but there are many places where OpenStreetMap might be the place for geodata to take on a life of its own.

The open data movement has grown in leaps and bounds over the last decade. With the expansion of the Internet, and spurred on by things like Wikipedia, SourceForge, and Creative Commons licenses, there's an ever-growing expectation that information be free. Some governments are rushing to meet this demand, and have become accustomed to making data open to citizens: policy documents, tax records, parcel databases, and the like. Granted, the prevalence of open information policies is far from universal, but the rate of growth of government open data is only increasing. In the world of commercial business, the encyclopaedia industry has been obliterated by the success of Wikipedia, thanks to the world's subject matter experts having an open knowledge platform. And GitHub's meteoric growth over the last couple of years is challenging how software companies view open source, convincing many to open source their code to leverage the power of software communities. Openness and collaborative technologies are on an unceasing forward march.

In the context of geographic data, producers struggle to understand the benefits of openness, and how to achieve the same successes enjoyed by other open source initiatives within the geospatial realm. When assessing the risk-reward of making data open, it's easy to identify reasons to keep it private (How is security handled? What about updates? Liability issues?), and difficult to quantify potential gains. As with open sourcing software, it takes a mental shift on the part of the owner to redefine the notion of "ownership" of the data. In the open source software world, proprietors of a project can often be thought of more as "stewards" than owners. They aren't looking to secure the exclusive rights to the access and usage of a piece of code for themselves, but merely to guide the direction of its development in a way that suits project objectives. Map data published through online portals is great, and is the first step to openness. But this still leaves an air gap between the data provider and the community. Closing this engagement loop is key to bringing open geodata to the same level of genuine growth and engagement that's been achieved by Wikipedia.

An innovative new approach to open geographic data is taking place today with the OpenStreetMap[52] project. OpenStreetMap is an effort to build a free and open map of the entire world, created from user contributions – to do for maps what Wikipedia has done for the encyclopaedia. Anyone can login and edit the map – everything from business locations and street names to bus networks, address data, and routing information. It began with the simple notion that if I map my street and you map your street, then we share data, both of us have a better map. Since its founding in 2004 by Steve Coast, the project has reached over 1 million registered users (nearly doubling[53] in the last year), with tens of

---

[52] http://openstreetmap.org/

[53] http://osmstats.altogetherlost.com/index.php?item=members

thousands of edits every day. Hundreds of gigabytes of data now reside in the OpenStreetMap database, all open and freely available. Commercial companies like MapQuest, Foursquare, MapBox, Flickr, and others are using OpenStreetMap data as the mapping provider for their platforms and services. Wikipedia is even using OpenStreetMap[54] as the map source in their mobile app, as well as for many maps within wiki articles.

What OpenStreetMap is bringing to the table that other open data initiatives have struggled with is the ability to incorporate user contribution, and even more importantly, to invite engagement and a sense of co-ownership on the part of the contributor. With OpenStreetMap, no individual party is responsible for the data, everyone is. In the Wikipedia ecosystem, active editors tend to act as shepherds or monitors of articles to which they've heavily contributed. OpenStreetMap creates this same sense of responsibility for editors based on geography. If an active user maps his or her entire neighbourhood, the feeling of ownership is greater, and the user is more likely to keep it up to date and accurate.

Open sources of map data are not new. Government departments from countries around the world have made their maps available for free for years, dating back to paper maps in libraries – certainly a great thing from a policy perspective that these organisations place value on transparency and availability of information. The US Census Bureau publishes a dataset of boundaries, roads, and address info in the public domain

---

[54] http://idealab.talkingpointsmemo.com/2012/04/wikipedia-drops-google-maps-for-openstreetmap.php

(TIGER[55]). The UK's Ordnance Survey has published a catalog[56] of open geospatial data through their website. GeoNames.org[57] houses a database of almost ten million geolocated place names. There are countless others, ranging from small, city-scale databases to entire country map layers. Many of these open datasets have even made their way into OpenStreetMap in the form imports, in which the OSM community occasionally imports baseline data for large areas based on pre-existing data available under a compatible license. In fact, much of the street data present in the United States data was imported several years ago from the aforementioned US Census TIGER dataset.

Open geodata sources are phenomenal for transparency and communication, but still lack the living, breathing nature of Wikipedia articles and GitHub repositories. "Crowdsourcing" has become the buzzword with public agencies looking to invite this type of engagement in mapping projects, to widely varying degrees of success. Feedback loops with providers of open datasets typically consist of "report an issue" style funnels, lacking the ability for direct interaction from the end user. By allowing the end user to become the creator, it instills a sense of ownership and responsibility for quality. As a contributor, I'm left to wonder about my change request. "Did they even see my report that the data is out of date in this location? When will it be updated or fixed?" The arduous task of building a free map of the entire globe wouldn't even be possible without inviting the consumer back in to create and modify the data themselves.

----

[55] http://www.census.gov/geo/maps-data/data/tiger.html

[56] http://www.ordnancesurvey.co.uk/oswebsite/products/os-opendata.html

[57] http://www.geonames.org/

Enabling this combination of contribution and engagement for OpenStreetMap is an impressive stack of technology[58] that powers the system, all driven by a mesh of interacting open source software projects under the hood. This suite of tools that drives the database, makes it editable, tracks changes, and publishes extracted datasets for easy consumption is produced by a small army of volunteer software developers collaborating to power the OpenStreetMap engine. While building this software stack is not the primary objective of OSM, it's this that makes becoming a "mapper" possible. There are numerous editing tools available to contributors, ranging from the very simple for making small corrections, to the power tools for mass editing by experts. This narrowing of the technical gap between data and user allows the novice to make meaningful contribution and feel rewarded for taking part. Wikipedia would not be much today without the simplicity of clicking a single "edit" button. There's room for much improvement here for OpenStreetMap, as with most collaboration-driven projects, and month-by-month the developer community narrows this technical gap with improvements to contributor tools.

In many ways, the roadblocks to adoption of open models for creating and distributing geodata aren't ones of policy, but of technology and implementation. Even with ostensibly "open data" available through a government website, data portals are historically bad at giving citizens the tools to get their hands around that data. In the geodata publishing space, the variety of themes, file sizes, and different data formats combine to complicate the process of making the data conveniently available to users. What good is a database I'm theoretically allowed to have a copy of when it's in hundreds of pieces scattered over a dozen

---

[58] http://wiki.openstreetmap.org/wiki/Component_overview

servers? "Permission" and "accessibility" are different things, and both critical aspects to successful open initiatives. A logical extension of opening data, is opening access to that data. If transparency, accountability, and usability are primary drivers for opening up maps and data, lowering the bar for access is critical to make those a reality.

A great example the power of the engagement feedback loop with OpenStreetMap is the work of the Humanitarian OpenStreetMap Team's[59] (HOT) work over the past few years. HOT kicked off in 2009 to coordinate the resources resident in the OpenStreetMap community and apply them to assist with humanitarian aid projects. Working both remotely and on the ground, the first large scale effort undertaken by HOT was mapping in response to the Haiti earthquake in early 2010. Since then, HOT has grown its contributor base into the hundreds, and has connected with dozens of governments and NGOs worldwide – such as UNOCHA, UNOSAT, and the World Bank – to promote open data, sharing, transparency, and collaboration to assist in the response to humanitarian crises. To see the value of their work, you need look no further than the many examples showing OpenStreetMap data for the city of Port-au-Prince, Haiti before and after the earthquake.[60] In recent months, HOT has activated to help with open mapping initiatives in Indonesia, Senegal, Congo, Somalia, Pakistan, Mali, Syria, and others.

One of the most exciting things about HOT, aside from the fantastic work they've facilitated in the last few years, is that it provides a tangible example for why engagement is such a critical

---

[59] http://hot.openstreetmap.org/

[60]   http://blog.okfn.org/2010/01/15/open-street-map-community-responds-to-haiti-crisis/

component to organic growth of open data initiatives. The OpenStreetMap contributor base, which now numbers in the hundreds of thousands, can be mobilised for volunteer contribution to map places where that information is lacking, and where it has a direct effect on the capabilities of aid organisations working in the field. With a traditional, top-down managed open data effort, the response time would be too long to make immediate use of the data in crisis.

Another unspoken benefit to the OpenStreetMap model for accepting contributions from a crowd is the fact that hyperlocal map data benefits most from local knowledge. There's a strong desire for this sort of local reporting on facts and features on the ground all over the world, and the structure of OpenStreetMap and its user community suits this quite naturally. Mappers tend to map things nearby – things they know. Whether it's a mapper in a rural part of the western United States, a resort town in Mexico, or a flood-prone region in Northern India – there's always a consumer for local information, and often times from those for whom it's prohibitively expensive to acquire. In addition to the expertise of local residents contributing to the quality of available data, we also have local perspective that can be interesting, as well. This can be particularly essential to those humanitarian crises, as there's a tendency for users to map things that they perceive as higher in importance to the local community.

Of course OpenStreetMap isn't a panacea to all geospatial data needs. There are many requirements for mapping, data issue reporting, and opening of information where the data is best suited to more centralised control. Data for things like electric utilities, telecommunications, traffic routing, and the like, while sometimes publishable to a wide audience, still have service dependencies that require centralised, authoritative management. Even with data that requires consolidated control by a government agency or department, though, the principles of engagement and short feedback loops present in the OpenStreetMap model could still be applied, at least in part. Regardless of the model, getting the most out of an open access data project requires an ability for a contributor to see the effect of their contribution, whether it's an edit to a Wikipedia page, or correcting a one way street on a map.

With geodata, openness and accessibility enable a level of conversation and direct interaction between publishers and contributors that has never been possible with traditional unilateral data sharing methods. OpenStreetMap provides a mature and real-world example of why engagement is often that missing link in the success of open initiatives.

Coleman McCormick is a geographer and software developer at Spatial Networks, Inc. in Clearwater, Florida, USA. With over 10 years experience in the mapping industry and a deep background in information technology, he creates and uses data and software products for geospatial applications. Coleman is an active contributor to the open mapping ecosystem, runs a regional OpenStreetMap community group, and enjoys spreading the word on open source software within students and universities.

Application

Thoughts on Open Innovation

Getting Requirements Right
Towards a nuanced approach on
Standardisation and IPRs

By Jochen Friedrich

Global ICT standardisation takes place in a diverse ICT standards ecosystem. Different organisations cover different technology areas. This includes a diversity of IPR policies – tailored by the members of the respective standards bodies so that the market is served best and innovation is promoted in an optimal way. Governments reflect this in their policy making when including a reference or requirements to standards and specifications. The differentiate between policy areas and the needs that evolve for standards supporting the respective actions. This level of differentiation leads to a nuanced approach which best serves the markets and unleashes the potential for innovation which can be achieved with the support of standardisation.

Introduction

Standards are the backbone of open ICT ecosystems. Standards facilitate market access by complying with basic regulatory requirements in the areas of health, safety and the environment. Standards are a key instrument for the broad adoption of new technologies. And standards enable and ensure interoperability and thus allow all market players to provide innovative technologies and compete on fair grounds. This is particularly critical for the combination of technologies in order to build new, innovative solutions. Prominent examples for innovations where technologies are integrated and therefore different standards are combined are Cloud, smart grid, smarter cities, etc.

Successful standardisation builds on two success factors: (i) the availability of technologies, i.e. the willingness of the owner, inventor or innovator to contribute their technologies to standardisation and thus make them available for broad exploitation; and (ii) the broad adoption of the standards on the global market place.

Both are also key aspects when looking at patented technologies. The intersection of IPR (Intellectual Property Rights) and standardisation is a complex and heavily debated area. Sometimes the debate seems to much to be held in black and white – especially in the context of the role of public authorities. This paper will give some perspectives on the topic and argue in favour of a nuanced approach.

Excursus: The Global ICT Standardisation Ecosystem

Standards bodies are to provide a platform for industry and other interested stakeholders to develop standards that suit the marketplace. Standards bodies are member driven and independent organisations.

There are formally recognised standards bodies, both on national, European and international level. These formally recognised standards bodies develop standards (norms) in so-called full-consensus processes, i.e. with broad and systematic stakeholder consultation in a public enquiry, and are in a position to provide standards/norms that are used in support of regulation. The binding rules for formal international standardisation are laid down in an Annex to the WTO TBT Agreement. In Europe the standardisation system is defined in a new Regulation which came into place on January 1, 2013 (1025/2012).

On the international level the three formally recognised standards bodies are ISO and IEC with the national formally recognised standards bodies as their members, i.e. BSI in the UK, AFNOR in France, DIN in Germany, etc. The similar structure exists for CEN and CENELEC in Europe. This structure includes that development of standards is done in a national delegation principle where national standards bodies set up mirror committees to the international or European projects and all mirror committees agree on delegates that are sent to the international or European level to represent the interests and decisions of the respective mirror committees. For the ICT sector ISO and IEC have established a Joint Technology Committee, the ISO/IEC JTC 1, where ICT standardisation takes place in the same way with national delegations.

For telecommunications there are ITU on the international level and ETSI in Europe. Both have different membership structures with national delegations where national governments have a key role in leading the delegations when it comes to developing formal standards. In ISO, IEC, CEN, CENELEC and in the national standards bodies the predominant business model is on selling the standards document. Abstracts – and sometimes pre-final drafts – are available publicly, but the final standards document is acquired from the standards body.

In Europe, the European Standardisation Organisations (ESO) have the explicit task to develop harmonised standards in support of the European common market. This concerns the areas health, safety and the environment which are governed in the New Legislative Framework in the EU including the New Approach Directives, e.g. the Directives on Product Safety, Electromagnetic Compatibility (EMC), Low Voltage (LVD). In short: In these areas the European Commission lays down the government requirements. Industry can voluntarily develop European

Standards (EN) in order to meet the requirements. Those who implement the respective standards therefore comply with the requirements on the basis of a presumption of conformity. The ENs are listed in the Official Journal of the EU.

In addition to this structure of formal standards bodies there are many other global standards bodies which, especially in the field of ICT (Information and Communication Technologies) develop global standards that are broadly used and implemented. Examples for such organisations include the IETF, W3C, OASIS, ECM international, OAGi, OMG, IEEE etc. The leading ICT standards bodies have broad global membership including all stakeholder groups and operate with open standards development processes that don't differ from the processes in the formal standards bodies. Some even may be regarded as having a higher level of openness and transparency based on the use of IT technologies and web tools. In W3C, for instance, all interested parties, whether members of the organisations or not, can follow the discussions and can give comments which are considered in the process.

It is fair to say that for IT technologies the private global organisations have the lead in developing the relevant global standards around the internet, the web, software and business processes. With some simplification it may be said that this applies for all areas that are relevant for the marketplace without affecting regulation in the areas of health, safety and the environment. When regulation comes to play some linkage with the formally recognised standards bodies and their processes is established. A prime recent example here is web accessibility where the respective W3C standard has been put forward via CEN for being eligible for referencing in EU regulatory contexts and for achieving a harmonised approach towards web accessibility –

harmonising across all EU member states and avoiding fragmentation.

There are some areas of technology where public interest exists to some extend and where, therefore, there is an interest in transposing specifications that were developed in private global organisations to the level of formal standards. Document formats are an example. Such standards and specifications may have relevance on a policy level outside of regulation. In order to accommodate the respective needs the leading global ICT standards bodies have created a liaison with ISO/IEC JTC 1 and have got PAS submitter status. PAS refers to "publicly available specifications" which means that organisations can submit their specifications directly for national voting and, thus, for adoption as a formal international standard.

Public authorities may trigger the development of standards or activities around standardisation in several ways. Regarding the use of standards in support of regulation the EU Commission may issue a Standardisation Mandate to the three ESOs in Europe. The ESOs evaluate the Mandate and propose respective work items. Notwithstanding, standardisation activities are voluntary and it is up to the stakeholders to decide whether to take up the work and engage in a standardisation activity.

According to the new EU Regulation on Standardisation (No 1025/2012) the EU Commission can also follow a process to identify global ICT specifications so that they can directly be referenced in public procurement. This allows for global Open Standards to be used and provides a basis for much broader adoption of global Open Standards by public authorities. Thus governments can further promote interoperability as well as competition via their power as a customer of ICT technologies and systems. And procurement plays a role in actually implementing government internal policies and thus strengthen policy making.

The Role of Standards Bodies regarding IPR

Standards Bodies need to have an Intellectual Property Rights (IPR) Policy which lays down the rules how IPRs that are included or critical for standards are dealt with. Typically such an IPR policy includes issues like which are essential claims?; when do they have to be declared?; what is the policy for licensing patents in standard?; until what point in time can a party opt out of a technical committee?; etc.

The IPR policy is developed by the members of the respective standards body. It needs to comply with basic law, e.g. patent law, competition law. Otherwise the members of the standards body are free to design a policy which suits their needs and ensures fair collaboration within the organisation.

With their IPR policies standards bodies thus ensure that patented technologies that are included in a standards are available for implementers. On a simplified level it may be said that for Information and Communication Technologies (ICT) the leading global standards bodies have chosen two models regarding the rules for patent licensing:

FRAND – Fair, Reasonable, Non-Discriminatory

FRAND is the model that has traditionally been applied in the context of technology. FRAND is a promise that members of a standards bodies give when declaring a patent as standards essential. It means that the respective patent holder is willing to license the patent to implementers on a fair and reasonable basis.

The actual negotiations between patent holder and licensee take place on a bilateral basis outside of the standards body.

The FRAND principle achieves that technical work on standards development can take place within the framework provided by the standards body. Commercial discussions are, as it were, kept out and therefore don't impact the technical work. The FRAND model has successfully been practiced for decades. This does not mean that there are no disputes. Disputes and impasses do occur once in a while and are usually dealt with in court or by arbitration. Yet, again, this happens outside of the actual standardisation environment and without direct impact on the standards bodies.

Royalty-free

The dominant model around technologies for the world wide web and for software interoperability is Royalty-free. The leading global standards bodies in this field have – based on the agreement of their members – implemented Royalty-free policies which require from the patent holders to license their patented technologies which are standards essential without compensation.

One Policy with Multiple Options

Some standards bodies have implemented a policy which includes different options so that it is possible to chose case-by-case between FRAND and Royalty-free. The most prominent example is OASIS. And even though over 90% of all OASIS standards have been developed by applying the Royalty-free option, the FRAND option is available and may be chosen in certain cases.

OASIS has also included another option which may be chosen – a non-assert commitment This means that patent holders commit that they will not execute their patent claims for the respective standard. This does, however, not mean that there is a general licensing on Royalty-free terms, but entirely circumvents the issue of licensing.

Diversity serving the Dynamics of the Marketplace

Diversity in standards bodies and in IPR regimes serves the market place with high success. It allows to apply policy approaches and rules in relation to specific markets and market needs. There is clearly no "one-size-fits-all" approach that would suit all technology areas and all purposes.

Industry and other stakeholders are, therefore, working jointly in different global standards bodies in order to develop the best IPR rules possible for the given technology area that is covered and addressed. Standards bodies are independent and sovereign bodies where stakeholders collaborate in open and transparent processes to reach consensus on what they find suits markets best. Competition that takes place between standards bodies on the global level further promotes a regular revision and transformation process including IPR policies. As a consequence this leads to constant improvements and adaptations to the needs of the market place.

Especially for a dynamically changing technology sector like ICT it is of high importance that standards bodies provide flexible platforms for best-of-class, market-driven standardisation. At the same time the presence of a broad spectrum of stakeholders in standards bodies balances out interests.

Innovation and IPRs

A major consideration for the choice of IPR policy in a standards body is how to best promote innovation. Both models described above, FRAND and Royalty-free, play an important role in promoting innovation in the context of standardisation.

Bringing base-technology into standardisation

It is essential to have new, patented, innovative base-technology available for standardisation. FRAND plays a key role here because it allows for compensation. This means via FRAND it becomes attractive for patent holders to bring in their patented technologies into standardisation. FRAND enables that patent holders will receive some reward for the efforts they have put in into Research and Development.

It is important to stress that the actual innovation in this case has taken place on the level of research and development activities preceding standardisation.

Innovation on the level of standards implementation

Standardisation as such is not normally innovative. Innovation mostly takes place on the level of the implementation of standards including the integration of technologies and the combination of standards. In this case the act of innovation takes place on top of the standards.

In order to promote innovation on the level of the implementation of standards the broad, global adoption of standards is important, if not a pre-requisite. Aspects like the availability of standards and the terms and conditions for their use are typically addressed and taken into consideration when working out requirements for IPR policies. Free availability of standards, e.g. for download on the web, and lack of IPR encumbrances for the use and implementation are, as it were, ideal factors on the extreme side for the update and adoption of standards. But they are not necessary factors for promoting the uptake. The most important factor, for sure, is market need.

Royalty-free – innovation in software

A boost of innovation took place over the last 15 years with the internet and the world wide web. This is innovation that takes place on the level of the implementation and combination of standards in the area of software interoperability. And all the innovation of the internet and the world wide web is based on so called Open Standards which are available Royalty-free. The standards have been developed in a couple of specialised global standards bodies. And there is broad agreement amongst industry and all stakeholders on the high importance of requiring Open Standards for software interoperability. This promotes the uptake and broad adoption of standards and thus makes them available for exploitation and for innovation. It also allows for implementation in Open Source and therefore promotes a level playing field in software interoperability.

Diverse patent policies in global standards bodies

A look at the different patent policies applied in global standards bodies shows that (i) there is a good deal of diversity amongst the leading IT standards bodies worldwide; (ii) that the choice of rules is taken in relation to the technology area where the key expertise of the standards body lies.

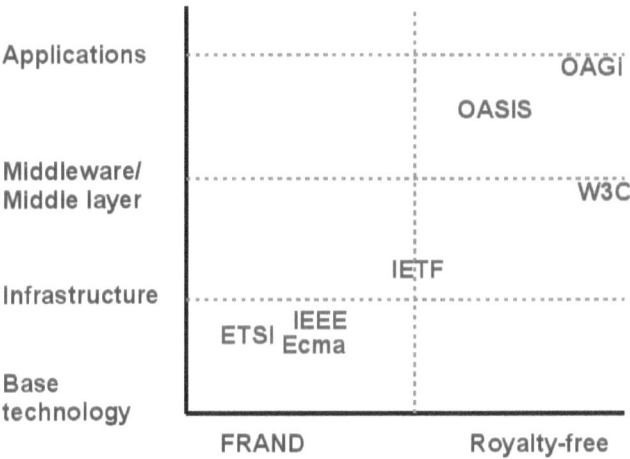

Figure 1: Global Standards Bodies and Patent Policies

On a simplified level it is fair to say that the higher-up in the stack, the more that software interoperability is concerned, the more has a Royalty-free patent policy been implemented. Figure 1 illustrated this picking some examples of the leading global internet and IT standards bodies.

It is on the middle-ware and application level where standardisation is about interoperability in software, about protocols and data formats. Royalty-free is the dominant model on this level. While for base technology, where innovation is largely in the technology components that are contributed to standardisation, that FRAND is the dominant model which has been chosen and implemented in patent policies.

Openness and Diversity

Openness is a major requirement in standardisation. But openness is not a clear cut state. It is rather a collection of requirements which should be met but which may be met to certain degrees, some in a more open way, some less. In other words, openness is some sort of continuum which starts beyond "closed" - which is clearly not part of the openness continuum – and extends into "fully open"with all requirements being met to the utmost.

Requirements or criteria to look at in the context of addressing openness in standardisation are (i) development process; (ii) maintenance; (iii) consensus building; (iv) availability; (v) rules for implementation.

Openness is, therefore, not contradictory to FRAND. Yet, there may be other criteria determining openness in certain contexts so that – depending on the area of technology – it may be appropriate to have different requirements on openness.

As explained above, one such area is software interoperability. It is important that software interoperability standards can be implemented in Open Source. This creates a level playing field for Open Source technology providers on the marketplace and makes the respective Open Standards available for broad adoption and thus promotes innovation that takes place on top of the standards.

The diversity of global standards bodies with different rules and policies that have been tailored to the specific needs of the stakeholders and the market is an ideal ecosystem for global standardisation in ICT. This also means that the global needs regarding innovation in relation to standardisation are best served with a diverse standardisation ecosystem.

Public Policy, Openness and Standardisation

As described above, there are different ways how standardisation and standards may be used in support of public policy. In a nutshell: standards ensure interoperability. They are key in providing a level playing field for competition and thus play a role in promoting openness, innovation and growth. Public authorities reap these benefits by referring to standards or demanding the use of standards in the context of public policies.

In Regulation, voluntary standardisation has proved to be an effective and efficient instrument in Europe for meeting regulatory requirements under a presumption of conformity. The respective standards that are used in the context of EU legal frameworks like Regulations or Directives normally need to be formal standards that have been developed with or adopted by the ESOs and their processes including in particular the formal public enquiry procedure. Broad consensus and an open, transparent and inclusive development process are key requirements which public authorities put onto the standards.

Another perspective is taken when innovation policy or industrial policy is concerned. In innovation policy public authorities usually wish to promote the adoption of new technologies in order to push innovation. This means, the broad availability of technologies is important and, in order to have a level playing field for competition, standards need to be implementable in Open Source when software interoperability is at stake. Therefore, governments typically take a strong stance in requiring Open Standards for eGovernment and software interoperability contexts. The Open Standards must have been developed in an open process and be available for implementation on Royalty-free terms and conditions.

Looking at innovation policy in other areas, e.g. where complex systems are concerned, the requirements need again be different – or better: more nuanced. Examples here are Smart Grid, eEntergy, eMobility, Intelligent Transportation, smart water supply etc. These are areas where technologies from different sectors are integrated which highly contributes to innovation of smarter ways and methods of how to do things. This integration of technologies is possible by combining the different standards into complex systems which address different levels of technology. It certainly remains a key requirement for the level of software interoperability that the respective standards should be Open Standards available for implementation on Royalty-free terms. Yet for other technology levels included, e.g. those where base technology is concerned, FRAND is the absolutely appropriate direction.

On the overall level, therefore, government rules need to be flexible and allow for the full spectrum of standards which have been developed in open processes to be available for referencing and use. Notwithstanding such a general framework, it is up to specific policies, e.g. in the area of eGovernment, to set their specific requirements to Open Standards. Such a nuanced approach will best serve different interests and objectives and will be the most effective way for promoting openness and innovation.

Concluding Remarks

The space between black and white is not grey but full of colours. It is important to be able to have access to all colours, to pick and chose the right ones for the right purpose and to combine the right ones into harmonious paintings.

The global ICT standardisation ecosystem provides an environment for standardisation that can serve the market needs in specific technology domains. Stakeholders all over the globe collaborate in the respective global standards bodies. This collaboration includes the agreement and improvement of IPR policies so that the respective organisation can work efficiently and produce best-of-class standardisation deliverables for broad market adoption.

In the context of public policy making, for standards that are used in support of public policy, it is important that specific requirements are made which meet the respective needs and can best support the policy objectives. Both, FRAND and Royalty-free have their role. FRAND is important for getting base technology into standardisation. Royalty-free is required in software interoperability in order to effectively promote innovation and competition and allow for implementation in Open Source. Bottom line: It is important to get the requirements right.

Jochen Friedrich is a member of IBM's Technical Relations Europe team which is part of the IBM Standards and open source Strategy organization. He is responsible for coordinating IBM's software Standardisation activities in Europe with a special focus on telecommunications, interoperability and services as well as on open Standards and the European Standardisation framework.

Jochen Friedrich Started his career in IBM at the Scientific Centre Heidelberg in 1998. Since then he has held several lead positions in Research and Development. He worked as operations manager for the IBM European Voice Technology Development team and was responsible for Business Development and Project Coordination for Voice Research projects in Europe. Jochen has broad experience in driving new, emerging technologies, managing multi-national and multi-company teams and setting up multi-company projects in the European Union research framework.

In addition to his IBM responsibilities, Jochen is a member of a regional board of the German Association of Electronics, Electrical Engineering and Information Technologies (VDE), he was a foundational Board member of the Enterprise Interoperability Centre (EIC) and holds lead roles in European induStry associations, moSt notably in the OpenForum Europe (OFE) where he chairs the Standardisation task force, in DigitalEurope (DE) and in the German ICT association BITKOM.

Jochen lives with his wife and two children in Heidelberg, Germany. He holds a PhD in Humanities from Heidelberg University (Germany), spent an academic year at Reading University (United Kingdom) and holds a degree as Certified Telematics Engineer.

Public Procurement: Free Software's Wild Frontier

By Karsten Gerloff

The Stakes

Public procurement makes up 19.4% of EU-wide GDP[61]. The public sector's procurement choices therefore have very real effects on the economy, and play a significant role in determining the sort of firms that thrive in the market.

Even with current procurement practices, Free Software[62] is already delivering very significant benefits to the European economy. Based on the evaluation of several code reuse surveys, Daffara (2012) estimates that Europeans enjoy 114 billion EUR per year in direct cost savings thanks to Free Software. In addition, reinvestment of these savings leads to an increase in

---

[61] Open Forum Europe (2013): OFE Procurement Monitoring Report 2012, 2nd Snapshot, p. 2. http://openforumeurope.org/openprocurement/open-procurement-library/Report_2012_2ndSnapshot\%20final.pdf

[62] http://www.gnu.org/philosophy/free-sw.html Free Software is sometimes referred to as "open source". While the terms encompass an identical set of licenses and programs, "Free Software" emphasizes the need for users to be in control of their computing, enabled by the freedoms to use, study, share and improve the programs they use.

productivity and efficiency worth at least 342 billion euro a year.[63]

Anecdotal evidence points in the same direction. To pick just some recent examples, the city of Arles (France) saved EUR 450,000 by replacing its proprietary database system with Free Software alternatives.[64] The Hungarian city of Miskolc reduced its annual cost per user by EUR 3,000 thanks to Free Software.[65] The regional government of the Canary Islands (Spain) was able to reduce its IT budget by 70% after deploying Free Software, saving EUR 700,000 over three years.[66]

On purely budgetary terms alone, there is thus a clear economic case to be made for Free Software both at the macro and the micro level. Free Software in the public sector is also crucial to ensuring that citizens are not forced to use non-free programs in order to interact with their governments. Free Software further secures strategic independence of public bodies' IT systems, and helps them break out of vendor lock-in.

Despite this evidence, most European public bodies continue to rely mainly on non-free software. Public procurement practices represent a major hurdle for the wider adoption of Free Software.

---

[63] Carlo Dafarra (2012): Estimating the Economic Contribution of Open Source Software to the European Economy. In: Shane Coughlan (ed.)(2012): The First OpenForum Academy Conference Proceedings, pp. 11-14

[64] https://joinup.ec.europa.eu/news/city-arles-pleased-savings-open-source-enterprise-software

[65] https://joinup.ec.europa.eu/elibrary/case/hungarian-city-miskolc-saving-%E2%82%AC3000-user-year-licenses

[66] http://joinup.ec.europa.eu/community/osor/news/canary-islands-save-70-cent-switching-open-source-virtualisation

We therefore need to investigate in which ways these practices fall short, and how they can be improved.

Minimum Requirements: Through The Floor

The minimum requirements for correct procurement practices are laid down in the Directive 2004/18/EC of the European Parliament and of the Council of 1 March 2004 on the coordination of procedures for the award of public works contracts, public supply contracts and public service contracts, in particular in Article 23(8):[67]

> *"Unless justified by the subject-matter of the contract, technical specifications shall not refer to a specific make or source, or a particular process, or to trade marks, patents, types or a specific origin or production with the effect of favouring or eliminating certain undertakings or certain products. Such reference shall be permitted on an exceptional basis, where a sufficiently precise and intelligible description of the subject-matter of the contract pursuant to paragraphs 3 and 4 is not possible; such reference shall be accompanied by the words "or equivalent"."*

The rule is clear: Procuring authorities must not refer to a trademark unless there is absolutely no other way to describe the sort of product or service they are seeking. In spite of this clarity, a substantial share of calls for tender systematically prevent companies offering Free Software from participating in calls for tender by making reference to trademarks.

---

[67]   See http://eur-lex.europa.eu/LexUriServ/LexUriServ.do?uri=CELEX: 32004L0018:EN:HTML

According to the latest regular procurement report by Open Forum Europe, during the period of October to December 2012, 19% of tendering notices made reference to trademarks.[68] Among the 148 notices containing trademark references, those references in 41 cases essentially said "the new product must be compatible with our current trademarked product".

Yet the other 107 notices explicitly to discriminate against other offers. In other words, roughly one in seven tender notices for software is anti-competitive.[69] The single most frequently used trademark was Microsoft's (in 73 notices), followed by IBM (in 21 notices)[70].

Keeping trademarks and other references to "a specific make or source" out of procurement notices is not optional; it is the minimum of neutrality required by European law. As the figures cited above demonstrate, this rule is frequently honoured more in the breach than in the observance.

Actual repercussions for the procuring authorities are rare. Many potential bidders rely on public bodies as a substantial source of business. In the absence of an effective anonymous complaints procedure, they are understandably loth to take steps which might alienate potential future customers.

---

[68] In total, 785 tendering notices were analyzed.

[69] Open Forum Europe (2013), pp. 8f.

[70] supra, p10.

Deficient Practices And Practical Solutions

In the following section, a series of case descriptions provide a basis for assessing both common problems in the public procurement of software, and potential solutions.

European Commission: Do As I Say, Not As I Do

A highly visible example of exclusionary practices in procurement was provided by the European Commission itself. In December 2010, one day before publishing a revised European Interoperability Framework urging European governments to build interoperable IT systems based on Free Software, the Commission decided in a closed-door meeting to extend its own use of of proprietary desktop operating systems and office productivity software.[71] Besides the more than 36,000 desktop computers at the Commission itself, 55 other European institutions were included in the contract.

When this decision was challenged by questions[72] from a member of the European Parliament, EC Vice-President Maroš Šefčovič argued that "[t]he Commission does not rely on (or is locked into) one single software vendor", citing the fact that the Commission's IT infrastructure uses software from many different vendors[73].

---

[71] http://www.nytimes.com/2011/01/27/technology/27msft.html

[72] See http://www.europarl.europa.eu/sides/getDoc.do?pubRef=-//EP//TEXT+WQ+P-2011-003807+0+DOC+XML+V0//EN&language=EN

[73] See http://www.europarl.europa.eu/sides/getAllAnswers.do?reference=P-2011-003807&language=EN

This reply, however, misses the point.[74] For one, the Commission was not looking for software in general. It specifically asked for an "office automation platform". Such a request is certainly "sufficiently precise and intelligible" in the sense of Directive 2004/18/EC Art. 23(8).

Šefčovič's claim that the Commission is not locked into any particular software vendor's offerings is led *ad absurdum* by the explanation he gives for avoiding a public call for tender:[75]

> *"A change of supplier would oblige the contracting authority to acquire equipment having different technical characteristics which would result in incompatibility or disproportionate technical difficulties in operation and maintenance."*

Šefčovič effectively argues that it would be just too difficult and expensive for the Commission to switch to a different supplier --- which is exactly the meaning of vendor lock-in. As a result, the European Commission and the other 55 institutions participating in the contract will now generate several years' worth more of files in secret, proprietary formats. This will drive them even deeper into lock-in, and will present a substantial barrier to choosing a different vendor (and perhaps even a Free Software solution) at the end of the current contract period.

---

[74] Karsten Gerloff (2011): The European Commission's locked-in syndrome. http://blogs.fsfe.org/gerloff/2011/06/06/the-european-commissions-locked-in-syndrome/

[75] supra

Ironically, Commission Vice-President Neelie Kroes pinpointed exactly this problem in a speech in June 2010:[76]

> *"After a certain point that original choice becomes so ingrained that alternatives risk being systematically ignored, no matter what the potential benefits. This is a waste of public money that most public bodies can no longer afford."*

The Helsinki Case: High Costs Or Lack Of Motivation?

The actual tendering process is only one building block in the process of adopting Free Software, and not necessarily the most important one. A crucial role is played by the competence and inclination of the relevant departments of the public body in question.

The public sector's complicated relationship with Free Software in procurement is not limited to the actual tendering process. The city of Helsinki provides an example of how a potential move towards Free Software can fail in the pilot stage despite the absence of technical problems.[77]

In January 2011, the Helsinki city council decided to conduct a pilot project in the use of the Free Software office suite OpenOffice. The program would be installed on the laptops of all 600 city board members. If the pilot was successful, a full roll-out to all 21,000 of the city administration's computers would follow.

---

[76] See http://europa.eu/rapid/press-release_SPEECH-10-300_en.htm?locale=en

[77] For a full discussion, see Otto Kekäläinen (2012): Executive summary and analysis of the Helsinki City and OpenOffice case in 2010-2011. http://fsfe.org/news/2012/news-20120412-02.en.html

During the pilot phase, users did not receive support from the city's IT department, and had to interact with the rest of the city's administration, which continued to use proprietary formats for document exchange. Even so, only 25% of users said in an email survey that they wanted to return to using the previous proprietary office suite.

At the end of 2011, the IT department distributed a report on the pilot to the city council. The report, a three-page document without any actual calculations, claimed that migrating to OpenOffice would cost the city EUR 21.5 million over a seven-year period.

According to the report, this cost figure was based on a "toolkit" provided by a consultancy firm. The Free Software Foundation Europe filed a freedom of information request asking for the formula by which the notional costs were calculated; that request was denied.

In preparing the report, the city's IT department obtained cost figures only from proprietary software vendors and resellers. Companies providing Free Software solutions were not contacted to ask for their cost projections.

The overall impression is that the IT department wanted to stick with its current proprietary solution regardless of the cost. The department created unfavourable circumstances for the OpenOffice pilot program. When the pilot was successful in spite of these obstacles, the IT department proceeded to prepare a report which was apparently biased in favour of the current solution. The denial of FSFE's freedom of information request indicates that the department would not be comfortable seeing its calculation methods discussed in public.

Similarly half-hearted attempts at self-justification are often used by public administrations that decide to abandon Free Software pilots or even full deployments, such as the German city of Freiburg[78] and the German Foreign Office[79]. Such course changes tend to coincide with changes in political control of the relevant organisation, rather than with any specific technical challenges.

Munich: The Thorough Approach

In contrast, the German city of Munich has long served as a prime example of a Free Software migration done right. The LiMux project has been discussed extensively elsewhere[80]. Crucial factors for the project's success are strong political backing and systematic planning of the migration. The city government also views the administration's use of Free Software as an important factor for developing the region's technological capabilities. Recently the project team has identified procurement as a crucial challenge, and is working to design procurement practices which are suited to the city's Free Software needs.

Sweden: Scaling Up

Public sector staff in both the IT department and in the procurement department may lack the knowledge even to know what to ask for. This adds to the difficulty of overcoming the challenges presented by entrenched suppliers.

---

[78] http://joinup.ec.europa.eu/news/advocacy-groups-decry-freiburgs-stealth-return-proprietary-office

[79] http://fsfe.org/news/2011/news-20110511-01.en.html

[80] e.g. https://joinup.ec.europa.eu/elibrary/case/declaration-independence-limux-project-munich-0

In contrast, an example from Sweden highlights how skilled procurement personnel with sector-specific expertise can deliver solid solutions and substantial cost savings.

One of Sweden's two central public sector procurement organisations, Statens Inköpscentral, in April 2011 published a framework agreement for Free Software and related services for the country's public sector.[81] This is likely the first such framework agreement in Europe, and possibly still the only one.

While most of the agreement consisted of standard language, some clauses were radically different. The procurement authority applied innovative and rigorous criteria in selecting the suppliers under the agreement. The selected suppliers would have to be able to supply both software under an OSI-approved license[82], and all important services related to the software, such as maintenance, migration, support and training.

The customers receive non-exclusive and indefinite rights to the software, including a right to copy, modify, correct, and further develop it. The customer has the right to hire third parties in order to utilise the software in accordance with the specified terms of use.

The supplier also must indicate to what extent the software license affects the customer's rights to the software. Suppliers are barred from imposing on customers any restrictions that go beyond the terms of the Free Software licenses involved. In addition, suppliers are obliged to make the source code for the resulting software publicly available on their website.

---

[81] Daniel Melin (Nov 12, 2011): Free Software in the Swedish public sector. Presentation at Free Software Conference and Nordic Summit, Gothenburg, Sweden. http://joinup.ec.europa.eu/sites/default/files/FSCONS_2011-11-12.pdf

[82] See http://opensource.org/licenses

Suppliers were carefully examined to determine their competence in the area for which they were bidding. Among other things, the successful bidders had to demonstrate their active participation in the upstream Free Software projects, both in terms of software contributions and involvement in the project's mailing lists.

Most of the procurement authority's framework agreements are challenged in court by unsuccessful suppliers. In the case of the Free Software framework agreement, there was no court challenge.

Among other things, this case highlights the important role of subject matter expertise in designing procurement actions. The framework agreement was only possible because the procurement authority had at its disposal staff who had both the necessary Free Software knowledge to develop and design innovative terms, and substantial experience in public procurement.

What Role For Policies?

Public procurement is subject to regional, national and European policies, and a number of governments and administrations have adopted policies calling for greater use of Free Software and Open Standards. However, it is doubtful whether these policies are making much of an impact in practice.

More recently, a number of countries have published policies relating to Free Software in the public sector, and to procurement in particular. For the most part, their implementation, where it is under way at all, is still in its early stages.

Netherlands

The Netherlands in 2007 released an "action plan", aimed at increasing interoperability through greater use of Open Standards, reducing supplier dependence through more use of Free Software, and promoting a level playing field in the software market[83].

While this policy has been widely referenced in discussions around Open Standards and Free Software, actual implementation in the Netherlands has fallen far short of expectations.[84] Paapst concludes that "the mere use of the legal instrument (e.g. the European procurement guidelines) is not enough to change behaviour"[85].

A clear demonstration of how substantially the Dutch policy has failed to take root is the attempt, in the fall of 2011, to deploy a mandatory online environment for all Dutch schools and students, based on the proprietary Microsoft Silverlight platform[86] – something which is clearly unacceptable under the official policy.

---

[83] Mathieu Paapst (2013): Barrieres en doorwerking : een onderzoek naar de invloed van het open source en open standaarden beleid op de Nederlandse aanbestedingspraktijk. Dissertation, University of Groningen. Available at http://irs.ub.rug.nl/ppn/353037710

[84] Indicating just how insignificant the policy has become, a recent overview of Free Software procurement policies (by a Dutch author, no less) fails to even mention the Netherlands: https://joinup.ec.europa.eu/software/studies/issues-open-source-procurement-european-public-sector-ii

[85] Paapst (2013), p206

[86] http://fsfe.org/campaigns/nledu/nledu.en.html

European Union

After a long and hard-fought discussion process, the European Commission published a revised European Interoperability Framework in December 2010[87]. The document aims to guide public bodies across all member states into making their IT systems more interoperable. Open Standards and Free Software are natural components of this effort.

Compared to the original European Interoperability Framework[88], published in 2004 by a public sector expert group, the new document uses an understanding of Open Standards[89] which is substantially watered down. In Action 23 of its "Digital Agenda", the European Commission also promises to "[p]rovide guidance on ICT standardisation and public procurement"[90]; a document to this effect is currently pending publication.

UK

Driven by austerity, the UK government has developed a relatively coherent set of policies relating to the procurement of Free Software, and the use of Open Standards in the public sector, such

---

[87] http://ec.europa.eu/isa/strategy/doc/annex_ii_eif_en.pdf

[88] http://www.fsfe.org/projects/eu/EIF-Brochure_corrected-web.pdf

[89] There is no universally accepted definition of what represents an Open Standard. Free Software Foundation Europe proposes a strong definition at https://fsfe.org/activities/os/def.en.html.

[90] See http://ec.europa.eu/digital-agenda/en/pillar-ii-interoperability-standards/action-23-provide-guidance-ict-standardisation-and-public

as the Government ICT Strategy (March 2011)[91] and a set of "Open Standards Principles"[92] (November 2012).

To appearances, these policies have not survived contact with reality. In January 2013, the UK government signed a framework contract with Oracle for GBP 750 million.[93] This was exactly the type of contract which was no longer considered acceptable. The UK policy has thus comprehensively failed its first big test. It remains to be seen whether implementation will improve with time, but there are substantial grounds for pessimism.

Portugal

Portugal is perhaps the European country which has gone farthest in this regard. In October 2012, the government published a list of Open Standards which public bodies will be required to use in future[94], as part of a broader Open Standards policy. This policy rests on a relatively strong definition of Open Standards[95]. It

---

[91] http://www.cabinetoffice.gov.uk/content/government-ict-strategy

[92] http://www.cabinetoffice.gov.uk/sites/default/files/resources/Open-Standards-Principles-FINAL.pdf

[93] http://blogs.computerworlduk.com/open-enterprise/2013/02/uk-government-fails-its-first-big-procurement-test/index.htm

[94] http://dre.pt/pdf1sdip/2012/11/21600/0646006465.pdf

[95] Under the definition, exclusive rights such as patents reading on the standard must be irrevocably made available royalty-free to the Portuguese state, but not necessarily to others.

remains to be seen what the impact of this policy will be in practice.

Basque Country

The Basque Country region in Spain has taken another interesting approach. It requires that all software developed for public bodies be published in a state-run repository under a Free Software license, in order to enable reuse by other public bodies and local companies.[96] Interestingly, this initiative was backed by local IT companies, who had observed how similar policies in other parts of Spain had helped companies in those regions to grow and develop valuable expertise.

France: Ayrault Memorandum

The Ayrault memorandum[97], released by France's prime minister in September 2012 and targeting the country's ministries highlights in detail the benefits of Free Software for the public sector. It:
- sets out a framework for inter-ministerial collaboration on Free Software development.
- calls for the creation of a network of experts to provide specific expertise to the administration.
- points to a framework contract for Free Software support, set up by the central procurement agency, which covers all ministries

---

[96]   http://blogs.fsfe.org/gerloff/2012/06/04/common-sense-in-the-basque-country/

[97]   http://circulaire.legifrance.gouv.fr/pdf/2012/09/cir_35837.pdf   English translation: http://www.april.org/en/french-prime-minister-instructions-usage-free-software-french-administration

- urges ministries to contribute 5-10% of their cost savings to the upstream Free Software products they are making use of, in order to enable further development of those products.
- orders ministries to remain in regular contact with important Free Software development groups in order to gauge the further course of development. The memorandum specifically names the Mozilla foundation (Firefox and other products) and the Document Foundation (LibreOffice).

Where most Free Software-related policies in EU member states provide a set of rules, which public bodies then may or may not follow, the Ayrault memorandum takes a uniquely practical approach. It provides a series of concrete measures to be taken, many of them assigned to a few specific ministries.

The memorandum is also unique in calling on public bodies to financially support the Free Software development groups which provide the programs used in the ministries.

Italy

In August 2012, Italy's parliament adopted some important changes to the country's Digital Public Administration Act ("Codice dell'amministrazione digitale"). In particular, it revised article 68, which deals with Free Software, open file formats and open data.

The article's new wording requires that before procuring non-free software, public bodies must demonstrate that it is impossible for them to use either a Free Software solution, or one that has been developed within the public sector.[98]

Free Software, as well as solutions developed in-house at a public body, thus legally take precedence over proprietary offerings.

Analysing the new text, Aliprandi/Piana (2013) conclude that:[99]

> *"To our knowledge, Italian law is the farthest-reaching law to date favouring the use of FOSS in the Public Administration and the general openness of their IT systems to create a public commons created by public money. The decision was made in a dire situation of the national economy and inspired by practical reasons (spending review) rather than idealistic ones. It seems however a new direction that can hardly be changed. Only it can be made less compelling by a slack implementation, if not outright non compliance. Vigilance is therefore required."*

How To Fix It

Policy makers, administrators, regulators and supervisors are currently failing to adequately address unfair procurement practices. This leads to serious distortions in the software market, making it even easier for entrenched software suppliers to keep

---

[98] Aliprandi, Simone and Piana, Carlo (2013) 'FOSS in the Italian public administration: fundamental law principles', International Free and Open Source Software Law Review, 5(1), pp. 43 – 50 DOI: 10.5033/ifosslr.v5i1.84. Available at http://www.ifosslr.org/ifosslr/article/view/84/150

[99] supra, p.6

their public sector customers locked into proprietary programs and file formats. Public administrations which make use of Free Software, on the other hand, are generally finding that things work as expected, if not better.

As a first step, public authorities need to ensure effective supervision of procurement practices. Procurement actions that fall short of legal requirements need to be fixed, and their retraction ordered if necessary.

Even slightly better monitoring might potentially lead to a significant improvement in procurement practices. For public bodies, procurement requires a significant effort. Having to retract a call for tender, due to complaints from either an excluded competitor or a supervisory body, is a worst-case scenario for many of those working in procurement. An increased risk of such "failure" due to complaints should therefore lead to a higher degree of compliance with the rules.

Monitoring could be improved by increasing the capacity of public sector supervisory bodies. In addition, governments could make independent monitoring of procurement more effective by increasing transparency (publishing more procurement-related data systematically and in open formats), and by giving independent monitoring bodies (whether run by the public sector or by civil society) legal standing to go to court over procurement actions which fall short of the legal requirements.

Frequently, however, legal deficiencies in procurement actions are not due to a desire to exclude competing offerings. Instead, they may stem from a lack of knowledge on the part of a public body's procurement and/or IT staff. This problem can be alleviated through clearer guidance from supervisory authorities and more frequent training of such staff on procurement-related issues. The costs for such measures will be quickly recovered through the savings generated by more competitive procurement processes.

Setting incentives for good procurement practices may also provide a cost-effective route to improvements. For example, the government of a country or region might award a prize for the best call for tender. Even a reward consisting mainly or exclusively of public recognition would likely prove attractive.

Policies can provide a helpful foundation for efforts by public bodies to improve procurement practices. It is however worth noting that many of the most successful instances of Free Software use in the public sector have occurred in the absence of an effective policy to incentivise them. This is true for both Munich and Sweden. In France, the Ayrault memorandum came at a time when Free Software was already widely used in many public sector organisations; the policy appears to be an effect rather than a cause of the significant use of Free Software.

What avenues are available to ensuring that such practices meet at least the minimal legal requirements of fairness, or perhaps even exceed them?

Policies still matter, because they lay the foundations for improved epractices on a broader scale beyond localised successes. Strong and clear requirements for Open Standards in public sector IT, as exemplified by Portugal, are an important first step.

The Swedish example shows what is possible when public bodies can make use of procurement staff with expert knowledge in both Free Software and procurement processes. It is safe to assume that if Sweden's Free Software framework contract was underpinned by a strong Open Standards policy, many more of the country's public bodies would make use of the arrangement.

In practice, public bodies considering a migration to Free Software are frequently faced with a veritable onslaught of lobbying from proprietary software vendors, who fear a loss of revenue. As Munich shows[100], strong and consistent political backing is a critical success factor particularly for highly visible migration projects.

Public sector organisations would further be well advised to consistently contribute a percentage of the budget savings which they achieve thanks to Free Software back to the groups developing the products which are being used. Far from being a charitable donation, this would constitute an investment to ensure the long-term development of these products. Such an approach would also give public bodies significant influence on the future direction of the product's development.[101]

Most of these measures are easy to implement. Their costs, if any, would soon be recouped several times over through the substantial savings they generate. All of them are well within the reach of governments determined to make IT spending more effective, curb the waste of public funds, and promote competition and fairness in the software market.

There is no shortage of ideas which are not only good, but already tried and tested in practice. All that is currently lacking for their wider adoption is political will.

------

[100] The city administration has certainly seen its share of lobbying, from a visit by Microsoft founder Bill Gates soon after the decision to migrate, to period bouts of publicity along the lines of "Munich's migration is failing". In fact, the project is fulfilling all expectations, and is on track for completion.

[101] Some private companies which rely on Free Software make this a regular practice.

Karsten Gerloff is the President of the Free Software Foundation Europe. FSFE's mission as an independent not-for-profit organisation is promoting freedom in the information society through Free Software.

In the course of this mission, Karsten Gerloff works together with developers, activists, business leaders and high-level political decision makers in order to create an environment where Free Software can reach its full potential as the foundation of a free digital society. He leads FSFE's participation in community and policy processes at the European and global level, and is a frequent speaker at a wide variety of conferences and events.

Karsten Gerloff has conducted extensive research on the economic and social effects of Free Software for the European Commission and other clients, and has led the development of training materials for Free Software entrepreneurs in Southern and Eastern Africa.

Understanding Commercial Agreements With Open Source Companies

By Amanda Brock

According to ZDNET's Dana Blankenhorn, most open source software no longer comes from open source developers, but from the proprietary companies. Having worked for 5 years as Canonical's General Counsel, heading up the legal team commercialising services associated with the Ubuntu operating system,[102] I was immersed in the hard work that comes with the commercialisation of open source software and been exposed to the models and tribulations of making money from FOSS. In this article I have taken some time to think about commercialisation as an issue and the models for commercialisation.

Collaboration and sharing are at the heart of open source development. The developers I have met - and I have met many - are in the main a beautifully idiosyncratic, highly intelligent and interesting group of free thinkers. Their inability to accept the parameters of current thinking seems to me to be key to the creativity they demonstrate in the technical solutions they develop. Combined with their idealism, it forms the basis of the thinking that allows them to challenge the logic of laws, such as IP and in particular copyright. Copyleft, developed as part of this free thinking, is a play on the legal term copyright and a great example of this.

---

[102] Amanda Brock is no longer part of the Canonical team. She has left her much loved Ubuntu to become a Director of the international technology law firm, Origin, www.origin.co.uk where she is able to support multiple FOSS developers and companies providing legal and strategy advice.

When I sat down to write this article, I looked online, as I always do. I am without doubt a victim of the Wikipedia culture. Having grown up without a computer and started my working life without the Internet, I am to this day, humbled by the vast sources of information sitting on open source software, in a technology based on that thinking. I can access this information from almost anywhere in the world. Information that, without thinkers like Richard Stallman, people whose motivation is not necessarily fame and money, but who are interested in making a better society through collaboration and the tools they can offer society, wouldn't be there for me or my research. Like people, whose strengths, if overplayed, become their weaknesses, the Internet may not always be a great thing, Wikipedia can be dangerous. How often have you looked up a sniff or sneeze to diagnose yourself with a serious illness.

In searching the terms Stallman and Copyleft on Google's search engine (which runs on server farms driven by open source software) I found a page[103] that Stallman had written for the GNU operating system.[104] A few things he says there really strike me as important. His opening lines, "Every decision a person makes stems from the person's values and goals. People can have many different goals and values; fame, profit, love, survival, fun, and freedom, are just some of the goals that a good person might have. When the goal is a matter of principle, we call that idealism. My work on free software is motivated by an idealistic goal: spreading freedom and co-operation. I want to encourage free software to

---

[103] http://www.gnu.org/philosophy/pragmatic.html

[104] http://www.gnu.org/, GNU is a Unix style operating system based on free software.

spread, replacing proprietary software that forbids cooperation, and thus make our society better."

Stallman refers to free software not open source. He is the father of the ideological free software movement. He goes on to say, "All code added to a GPL-covered[105] program must be free software, even if it is put in a separate file. I make my code available for use in free software, and not for use in proprietary software, in order to encourage other people who write software to make it free as well. I figure that since proprietary software developers use copyright to stop us from sharing, we co-operators can use copyright to give other co-operators an advantage of their own: they can use our code."

Not all code in the world of free and open source software is copyleft. The term is not enshrined in law, but a pun from this man, this free thinker. Its symbol is a reverse of the copyright symbol ©. For those not so familiar with it, "Free software" means software that respects users' freedom and community. Roughly, the users have the freedom to run, copy, distribute, study, change and improve the software. With these freedoms, the users (both individually and collectively) control the program and what it does for them." The GNU web site goes on to say ""free software" is a matter of liberty, not price. To understand the concept, you should think of "free" as in "free speech," not as in "free beer"." The essence of "free" software is enshrined in the concept of Copyleft.

As a concept, copyleft takes copyright (where the creator of a work is the owner of the copyright in code they develop and third

---

[105] GPL – the GNU General Public License, is an OSI approved standard open source license published by the Free Software Foundation ("FSF") on the terms of which free software may be distributed by anyone who meets the free software definition and complies with the license terms.

parties may use it only with the owner's consent) and turns it around. It does so by requiring that both the work created and licensed for free use and any changes made to it by a third party are subject to the same ongoing freedoms and that this freedom cannot be restricted without the owner of the original copyright works consent.

To make this concept a reality Stallman and his advisers developed a tool in the licence of free software, which is what most lawyers are referring to when they say that a software licence is copyleft. The copyleft tool is simply a licence provision that ensures that any user who takes and modifies the code they received under a free licence will, if they distribute the modified code, do so under the same free licence without any additional restrictions or conditions and will release the source code in what is distributed under those original terms. The GNU General Public licence is probably the best known and most used example of this type of licensing.[106] Each party will own the copyright in what they have created but must license any new or modified version of the code under the same terms as the code they received, i.e. the licence being copyleft, the rights are left in the free code and the quid pro quo for usage is that new developments must be contributed back.

The licence terms allow anyone to modify and extend the code subject to this restriction included by the guardians of free software for the user's own safety. It intends to preserve the

---

[106] GPLv2 section 6. Each time you redistribute the Program (or any work based on the Program), the recipient automatically receives a license from the original licensor to copy, distribute or modify the Program subject to these terms and conditions. You may not impose any further restrictions on the recipients' exercise of the rights granted herein. You are not responsible for enforcing compliance by third parties to this License.

freedom under which the software was initially distributed through the use of copyleft.

As the creator of the original work owns the copyright in his work, despite the work being licensed under a copyleft licence for use by others, should any user not contribute back under the same licence, then they would have stepped beyond their rights under the licence and potentially be in breach of the original copyright holder's rights.[107]

Copyleft code when combined in certain ways with other code may create a new collective piece of code which is in fact a derivative work. It's like cracking eggs to make an omelette. Once the eggs are combined they become one new thing not individual eggs. That doesn't mean to say that there are not ways of putting together a new meal with the eggs without mixing them and in which the eggs stay as individual eggs, like gammon with a lovely fried egg on top. But, once they are mixed together to make an omelette, they are combined to create a new and distinct thing, like a derivative work.

Where this happens the new derivative work, like the original copyleft licensed component, will also be subject to copyleft terms. This impact of copyleft has been referred to as a "viral effect", where the free copyleft software, if combined with other code to create a derivative work, "infects" the other code with its freedom. It is something which has created considerable fear in the minds of owners of proprietary code and is perhaps the biggest single factor that dissuades some business usage of free

---

[107] GPLv2 section 4. You may not copy, modify, sublicense, or distribute the Program except as expressly provided under this License. Any attempt otherwise to copy, modify, sublicense or distribute the Program is void, and will automatically terminate your rights under this License. However, parties who have received copies, or rights, from you under this License will not have their licenses terminated so long as such parties remain in full compliance.

software. In short the owners of proprietary code are scared to use free software. They are afraid that the copyleft code will virally effect their own code.

Copyleft code is therefore seen to be subject to restrictions around how it may be distributed and how it may be combined with other code.

Clearly this sits well within the ideology Stallman espouses. His copyleft ideology creates a cascade of free software and freedom. As a paternalistic concept, it protects users from themselves in the interest of freedom. The consequences of copyleft are not an accident, but a carefully crafted attempt to preserve this freedom and remove temptation.

This ideology is akin to political thinking as opposed to software coding. The decision to create this was not a technological or development decision, but the expression of a belief system. That belief system is the centre of free software and the free software movement.

Its principles offer little space for commercialisation of free software. Freedom does not however necessarily mean that no price can be charged for the code and states in GPLv3, in section 4 which deals with distribution or conveying software, "You may charge any price or no price for each copy that you convey, and you may offer support or warranty protection for a fee."

The term open source was adopted in 1998, by a group on the US's West coast. The adopters formed a movement that is younger than free software and rejected some of the free software philosophy. Eric Raymond and Bruce Perens founded the Open Source Initiative later that year.[108] Its foundation was, to some extent at least, a reaction against the values of free software.

---

[108] http://opensource.org/history

Like free software, open source software involves the distribution of the source code in software. This means that the human readable secret sauce that allows people not machines to understand and read software, is freely available with the binary computer readable code in any software distributed in this way. This allows users to access the functionality of the code as you would with software distributed on a proprietary basis and also gives access to the methodology of the code that is seen in the source component. It allows recipients of the code to modify, extend and maintain the code themselves, if they have the appropriate skill set. This is different from proprietary software distribution where the source is secret and is akin to free software distribution where the source is shared. This ability to allow software developers to work together on code is the collaboration at the core of open source.

In the same way as the FSF have a set of criteria to be adhered to in the definition of free software, the Open Source Initiative ("OSI") created a definition that sets out 10 criteria to be met to be able to call software "open source". Like free software there is no legal constraint on anyone calling their code either free or open. However, if you wish to comply with the true sense of either meaning then a distributor should meet the criteria set out by either the FSF free software definition or the OSI's Open Source Definition ("OSD").

There are differences in the two groups' criteria and definitions. These differences are based on the ideological differences between the two groups. Open source may be considered to be a more pragmatic approach to software freedom, one that is more acceptable to business and which focuses less on ideology and more on pragmatism. By 1999 the OSI had approved its first list of licences as meeting its OSD. Today the OSI has approved a large number of licences. Its licence review process and the OSD have become an industry standard for open source licences with the OSI taking on the mantle of a standards body. In its work over the years, the OSI has tried to keep this simple and avoid licence proliferation[109] by reducing the number of licences and categorising licences into groups.

Within the OSI's mission statement it says "Open source is a development method for software that harnesses the power of distributed peer review and transparency of process. The promise of open source is better quality, higher reliability, more flexibility, lower cost, and an end to predatory vendor lock-in". A commercially focused statement, geared to attract business to open source, by setting out a list of some of open source's attributes and the associated business benefits. A far cry from Stallman's free software ideology! This lacks the paternalistic approach of protecting both freedom in code and users from themselves.

Whilst there are clear ideological differences there are not so many practical differences between the two groups. One of the key practical differences is the existence of permissive licensing through the OSD. A permissive licence is one that has few requirements around how the software licensed under it may be distributed and allows wide usage of the code. It allows distribution on an open basis but does not require the copyleft or share-alike contribution back of modifications and which may allow for modified versions of the code to be distributed under a

---

[109] The name given to the large volume of approved licenses for open source software which had been approved by the OSI, some of which were neither popular nor frequently used, which had terms which might not be compatible with other approved licenses and the volume of which caused confusion.

different or modified licence. Examples of licences that are permissive include the Apache,[110] BSD[111] and MIT licences.[112]

Permissive licences, such as the BSD do not require derivative works to be distributed under the same licence terms as the original code and allow additional or different licence terms to be added to the modified version of the code. Whilst they require an acknowledgement of the author in the code's notices they do not meet the enforced protection on long-term freedom Stallman sought in his copyleft approach. The width of the licence means that the user has choices that may, arguably, give the individual more freedom in how they use and distribute the code, but which remove the collective freedom enshrined in the copyleft principle. The FSF is concerned that permissive licensing does not protect freedom.

In the case of BSD distributed code, the code can be re-distributed under other terms and could even be taken into proprietary code without infringing the original licence of the code. As the code can be incorporated into a copyleft piece of code, it is GPL compatible and so can be combined with software meeting the free software definition. However, code released under the GPL could not be combined into a BSD licence as this would have the effect of changing the licence and be a breach of the GPL licence. Where code is copyleft, a licence cannot be

---

[110] http://www.apache.org/licenses/

[111] http://en.wikipedia.org/wiki/BSD_licenses

[112] http://en.wikipedia.org/wiki/MIT_License

changed without the consent[113] of the creator of that code. A significant problem in the existence of the two groups is that not all permissive licences approved by the OSI may be suitable for combination with copyleft software licences.

Ideologically the free software and open source movements see themselves as being quite far apart. From the outside looking in this may be very confusing and even seem a little nonsensical. Both movements distribute software that has freely available source code. The difference to any user would lie purely within the terms of the licence chosen for the software's distribution. The user may well not care what the licence terms are. They will only really be interested if the terms have any impact on them. Only users who play with the code by modifying it or combining it with other code are likely to care what the licence terms say.

So, at the start of this chapter I said I would write about the commercialisation of FOSS (free and open source software). Why am I hung up in history? As I started to think about the issues and explaining how I see them I realised that the only way to fully explain them is to work through this thought process. So, understanding where the players in FOSS have come from is important.

I suggest that having thought about the legal and ideological context, we look more generally at how organisations make money from FOSS (Free and Open Source Software). In both definitions a fee can be charged, so there is nothing to stop you

---

[113] GPL section 10. If you wish to incorporate parts of the Program into other free programs whose distribution conditions are different, write to the author to ask for permission. For software which is copyrighted by the Free Software Foundation, write to the Free Software Foundation; we sometimes make exceptions for this. Our decision will be guided by the two goals of preserving the free status of all derivatives of our free software and of promoting the sharing and reuse of software generally.

there. Ideologically, commercialising free software, may not sit well with the FSF and Richard Stallman's ideological goals, but it is not prohibited. Why however would anyone pay for software that they can generally receive free as in beer not just in speech? The answer is that they are likely to save their money for that beer and instead download the software for free. So, what is it that they might pay for? A very good question.

The question's ultimate answers may in fact have been delayed by the good intentions and philanthropic actions of a few large companies and wealthy individuals who have recognised the potential for the greater good in open source and so have offered massive resources to the infrastructure both through pure financing and also through their contribution of employee time and business assets such as patents. IBM is a major contributor to open source. It was a founding member of the Open Invention Network ("OIN")[114] patent pool. The patent pool is free to license and offers licensees the protection of not being sued by patent contributors and fellow licensees who offer cross commitments not to sue on their patents where those patents read on software that falls within the OIN Linux definition. Their contribution to open source has been massive and this type of generosity has played a significant part in the sustainability of FOSS over a number of years. As the market matures, however, so must the funding.

The simplest and most recognised answer to that question in a young market is of course the provision of related and specialist services. Just because the software is free doesn't mean that it is guaranteed. Many FOSS licences expressly state that the software comes without warranty. So, if you want to ensure that the software works either generally or in a specific context, you may

---

[114] http://www.openinventionnetwork.com/

wish to engage the services of a software engineer or a software engineering company to work on that code. They may check it, modify it and develop it further for you. If the code is copyleft, you may have to share your changes if you distribute the code. If you keep it for internal usage you may not have to. If the code is on a permissive licence, you may be able to keep that code or even distribute it without resorting to the original licence terms.

Free software purists may not be happy with your actions as they do not sit well with the ideology of free software with changes being contributed back for the greater good, but there is nothing to stop you keeping the code in house and benefiting from the free or open source software code it was based on. There are many examples where companies, even those considered good citizens in the world of open source have done so. They have utilised freely distributed code, modified it for their own business purposes, kept the modified code for their own usage and received huge cost benefits in doing so. As they do not distribute the modified code copyleft requirements do not kick in.

As server based services such as cloud computing or big data may not involve the distribution of code but the utilisation of services from servers running FOSS code, many companies have benefitted from FOSS software to build their server side services and now sell those services to third parties without passing on the code itself. In this way they may sell highly profitable services based on FOSS software without making a contribution back or serving Stallman's greater good.

As well as buying development services from open source software developers the code can be commercialised server side. As individuals and businesses use these services, purchasing them through an on line process in many cases, we have become increasingly used to contracting for these on a click through basis. This is creating a market place where users may not properly review the terms and conditions that they sign up to. For providers of these services, to ensure that the terms are enforceable its important to ensure that they are fair and fall within the legal parameters of what can be excluded. Where exclusions need to be drawn to the end user's attention this should be done carefully. There is also a risk that the infrastructure utilised is so closed down that even for bigger contracts the opportunity to negotiate is in fact removed. If this is the case the providers may be storing up long term problems for themselves depending on how much they try to exclude, certain exclusions being potentially contrary to legal requirements with respect to fairness if they are not open to negotiation.

Commercial use of the code may be a little more difficult where the mode of commercialisation is device rather than server based. In this instance, the code may be freely downloaded and utilised on a consumer or business device. The code may be pre-loaded onto the device or downloaded across the airways via a repository on boot of the device. Updates are generally provided in this later way via repositories. The code is still warranty free and may however not be suitable for either a particular device or particular usage of that device without some work. That development work may be done in house or provided by a third party and may be subject to a requirement to contribute the development back depending on the licence type, i.e. copyleft.

The consumer focus of certain devices may also create concerns in larger organisations where there are cascades of existing consumer terms and processes that may not be compatible with every FOSS licence. In these environments it may be necessary for the organisations to adopt licence preferences in their Open Source Policies and to check that the licences in the software coming into their organisations for onward distribution meet their compliance and policy needs.

However usage on the client side where the user interface ("UI") of the code is visible, as it is with software loaded on end user devices as opposed to servers, may encounter one of the more current and controversial legal issues in FOSS, trade marks. Where a brand or trade mark is associated with FOSS software, whilst the code may be freely used, whether and how the brand or mark may be used by a third party is dependent on the owner's trade mark policy. Some brands may require payment for a trade mark licence, others may require that the code is used as is or the brand removed. The owners of trade marks are within their rights to do so and commercial usage which will involve brands and marks should be carefully considered as there may be both a brand usage and cost consideration in doing this. It is of course possible to remove the brand or trade mark from the code and to distribute the code. In some instances that could provide a solution, but for other software, part of the reason for using it will be the user confidence created by the brand and it would certainly be detrimental to remove that brand or mark which inspires user confidence.

In some instances the code developer or sponsor may own other intellectual property rights such as design rights or design patents that will be subject to similar provisions. Again, this is relevant only in devices where the branding is seen, i.e. client software and not on the server side.

In addition to development services, software may require ongoing support and open source software companies will frequently offer to sell such support services. These services vary from being a pure service provision where the updates to the software are already provided free of charge, to a subscription model where the updates are provided only where support services have been purchased.

These add-ons to open source software are now almost a traditional route to the commercialisation of open source software. The ability for companies to make money from these depends on many commercial factors such as the popularity of the underlying software. Red Hat has become very well known as one of the most successful open source companies and in 2012 became the first open source company to generate over $1billion in annual revenue. Their model includes providing support, training and integration of their Red Hat Enterprise Linux ("RHEL") software. This is a subscription model where updates to RHEL are available only via this subscription. Their Fedora operating system offers a free community based alternative to this and much of the Fedora development may make its way into the RHEL product.

The trade mark concern has raised its head with RHEL. CentOS provides a free operating system with its upstream distributor, RHEL. CentOS are able to take the freely available RHEL distribution and use the source code to create an operating system which is very similar to RHEL. Notably the RHEL trade mark is not utilised in the CentOS distribution.

1Red Hat is a leader in this pack. It's the first open source company to generate an annual revenue of $1billion and whilst many open source companies would like to snap at its heels, this is a difficult proposition.

1Google and other search engines that generate revenue from advertising also play a part in the commercialisation of open source software. The revenue generated in their advertising deals not only provides these organisations themselves with revenue but this revenue is shared throughout an ecosystem of toolbar distributors and browsers who contribute to the traffic flow. This form of revenue can be very lucrative to open source companies that distribute code client side and is very dependent on volume of users.

We live in a time and world of disruptive forces in technology. The Android mobile phone operating system is a good example of market disruption being caused by open source software.

The late Apple founder, Steve Jobs' biographer Walter Isaacson has quoted Jobs as saying ""I will spend my last dying breath if I need to, and I will spend every penny of Apple's $40 billion in the bank, to right this wrong," Jobs told his biographer. "I'm going to destroy Android, because it's a stolen product. I'm willing to go thermonuclear war on this." And so began one of the biggest battles of my life time, the Android patent wars. They are easily the subject of a book and I don't want them to dominate this article. So, I will keep it short. Apple and Microsoft have alleged that the Android operating system infringes various patents held by them. They have attacked makers of android devices in multiple patent suits in various jurisdictions. The free nature and popularity of the android mobile OS has caught consumer imagination and very few users will not have seen the ensuing press following this litigation. It has been brought well and truly into the public eye.

The nature of patents in software and number of patentable pieces of code in any smart phone device, including Samsung and HTC, means that it is very easy for patent owners to sue and be counter sued. The extent of this war of litigation has led many people to ask me who can win from all these counter suits but the lawyers charging tens of millions of dollars to litigate these suits. Frankly, I am not sure that I can disagree with this analysis although some of the patent holders who are trying to charge a royalty per device could become winners.

In short the patent litigation creates a risk to open source as it may carry two consequences. Firstly if the litigation was successful the patent holders might be in a position to charge a royalty that in effect could create a premium on the cost of open source usage. Secondly it could enforce a barrier to entry, where users are put off the usage of open source due to fear of litigation. However, my personal view is that, this will not ultimately be successful. The continued success of the Android phones in the smartphone market place, sharply followed by Mozilla and Canonical's mobile OSs may be a good indicator of the ongoing force of open source that is moving in this direction. The existence of the litigation itself could arguably be considered to be nothing more than evidence of the success of open source's commercialisation in this way and the ongoing fear being caused in the established market places in which it is competing.

Android is clearly on of the most disruptive forces to create waves in a market place. However, I am seeing ongoing waves of disruption that may not be a tsunami, but over time may build up to one. These involve the creativity of multiple organisations seeking forms of funding not only to be profitable but going back to Stallman's thoughts on decision making, where actions are motivated by various reasons including the individuals' values. For some individuals and organisations that would be generating profits and meeting share holder value, but for others in the open source space, it may be as simple as paying for their own excellence, i.e. being able to generate enough revenue for sustainability.

Disruptiveness and that approach thinking outside of the box of convention may be much wider than looking to software for profitability. Emerge Open is a UK company that was formed was to find sustainable means of funding for Open Source projects. Despite accepting the current necessity for donations the founders are working on getting models to pay for their sustainability off the ground. IT Recruitment is a market worth tens if not hundreds of billions globally. As one of Emerge Open's directors is from a recruitment agency background, they are working on a model where recruitment agent services will be provided and function just like a normal recruitment agency but all the profits will go to funding Open Source projects. In doing so they are using the considerable pool of open source talent to specialise in a space that is well known to them, but where they offer customers the added value that the profits made by their business will go back into the market sector, i.e. open source.

App stores have become a massive part of software distribution. Apple and other smart phone companies have created a very profitable, although potentially transient market place for their profit in distributing native apps (apps designed or modified to work on their devices, develop or modified through their APIs and for sale or distribution from their stores). The reason that this may be a potentially transient model is the improving functionality of HTML5 and other coding tools which make Web Apps better. As Web App functionality improves, the lives of developers will become easier with Apps being able to work across devices without the need for tailored development. Whether Web or native is the final route, running an App store may be a great source of profit. Contributing Apps for distribution through those stores may also be a source of profit. There are some issues however with respect to the infrastructure of App stores including the terms and conditions being put in place.

In the early analysis we worked through the issues which copyleft may raise and of course the fact that there may not be additional terms and conditions added to the code's licence if it is a GPL one. This could easily not be an issue but unfortunately some App stores have not simply ring-fenced the code and its licence terms with the store's terms being restricted to terms of usage and sale. Where App stores have not taken adequate care to ensure that their terms do not add extra conditions to the licence or have otherwise not complied with licence requirements e.g. providing access to the source code or allowing modifications to be licensed back on the same terms, the licence may be infringed by the app store's distribution. The theory would be that this is not an issue as the developer who owns the app must have put it onto the store for distribution under the licence, knowing the terms that the store imposed and would not do so if they were unhappy with it. If the store's terms changed over time the developer could always remove the app. Some may take the view that an unenforced copyleft licence is no different from a permissive licence, but there is no obligation on a developer to enforce their licence copyleft of otherwise.

The collaborative nature of open source can however be problematic in this situation. If the app is being distributed in a potentially infringing way, then the collaborative nature of development and the fact that it is unlikely that one individual created a piece of code, and even if they appear to then others code is likely to interface with it, may prove problematic. Apple felt the wrath of the FSF who own the copyright in some of the VLC media player's code (it having been assigned to them by developers under their contribution agreement). However, their response to the FSF may seem to many to have backfired from an open source perspective. Rather than fight the issue, they simply removed the GPL code from their app store in response to the threatened litigation. They were able to do so by relying on the safe harbour provisions of the US copyright legislation under which they are merely a publisher. This reaction appears to be perfectly legal but did not enhance the reputation of open source, nor fix the potential conflict between the Apple app store and GPL.

There are undoubtedly many, many ways to commercialise open source software. Some are more obvious than others. Some are more problematic than others. The question of course will be how successful will they be and whether they can sit with the ideological stance taken by the early developers of free software, to allow for funding the long term sustainability of FOSS. At this stage in time, that remains to be seen. What is clear however is that the commercialisation of FOSS comes with technical, legal and ideological issues which will certainly impact its success.

There is no such thing as a free lunch. Is there such a thing as a free piece of code?

Amanda Brock advises a diverse group of companies on commercial and technology law issues from her London base. Having been General Counsel, Canonical – lead commercial sponsor of the open source operating system Ubuntu, for 5 years, where she managed the worldwide legal function she has particular expertise in open source software, cloud computing, big data and device manufacture and distribution.

With over 15 years experience of commercial and IT law, gained working as an in house lawyer, including roles as European Manager at DSG International where she was the first lawyer at the ISP, Freeserve (UK's first and biggest .com IPO), UK Legal Director, Aramark and General Counsel Nicole Farhi & French Connection, she has diverse experience which lends to her very commercial approach to legal advice.

Amanda is as a solicitor , admitted in England and Scotland and has a Masters in IP and IT law from Queen Mary and a Masters in Comparative Jurisprudence from NYU. Amanda is a member of the Advisory Board of the QM, University of London Open Source Centre of Excellence and has spoken internationally and written extensively on Tech and commercial law. She is one of the founders of the QM Legal Incubator currently being set up to provide legal advice to the UK start up market place. Her clients range from start ups to Mozilla.

Things To Come

Thoughts on Open Innovation

No One Speaks For Me
The Legislative Disconnect Of The Meshed Society

By Simon Phipps

What is the "meshed society"? It is people, joined together by the Internet, able to interact -- to collaborate, to create, to transact and to relate directly with each other -- without the need for another person to mediate. As we discover more and more ways to disintermediate our interactions, society is transformed: from a series of hubs with privileged interconnections intermediating supply to consumers, into a constantly shifting "adhocracy".

In the adhocracy, individuals play the roles of user, repurposer, maker, buyer and collaborator in a constantly changing spectrum of combinations. But the law, gathered as it has around the hub-and-spoke worldview of the industrial society, treats many of these roles as privileged, because they have historically been reserved only for commercial entities. Thus, individuals run afoul of rules intended to regulate the owners of hubs. Worse, the penalties associated are disproportionate with the acts they address, because they are designed as disincentives for industrial gaming -- not the human-scale actions of the meshed society.

This is toxic for innovation. Facing the changes of the meshed Internet society by merely tweaking the rules of the industrial society will fail; instead, we need to fully refactor those rules to account for the new topology of society.

As I have watched several bills be presented to various legislative assemblies I have been struck by the absence of any voice within the legislative process itself that speaks for my needs as an individual citizen in the meshed society of the 21st century. The Regulation of Investigatory Powers Act (RIPA), the Digital Economy Act (DEA), the Anti-Counterfeiting Trade agreement (ACTA), the Communications Data Bill (CDB), the Trans-Pacific Partnership Agreement (TPP) -- all have appeared apparently from nowhere replete with terms that poison the Internet collaboration of creator-consumer citizens who are unable to fully participate in the lawmaking process.

While the needs of the entertainment industries, of technology corporations, even of newspaper magnates seem well understood -- along with most other corporate concerns -- the outlook and needs of the individual writer, maker, technology entrepreneur and citizen-journalist seem entirely absent from the discussion. Even the voices of "civil society" frequently seem to speak only for the consumer and never for the individual creator-consumer. The government has civil servants, police and military intelligence all speaking in favour of draconian restrictive and secretive legislation, and is consulting the "Internet industry".

But who speaks for me? Shouldn't the politicians be representing me? Should citizens really have to pay for specialists to prevent the government infringing their rights and damaging their futures? Innovation depends on this ever-shifting interaction between citizens in their Internet roles, so a legislative world where their voice is absent could turn into a rolling disaster for society. To understand how the individual creator-consumer has ended up voiceless, it helps to understand the industrial roots of the existing process.

The Industrial Society

The industrial revolution accelerated an effect that was already in progress: concentrating the production into just a few hands with the rise of the factory; concentrating distribution into fewer hands through the rise of canals and then railways; and, concentrating control of communications into the hands of government-created monopolies of state. The social origins of many entrepreneurs, combined with the pollution created by factories, forced their location away from traditionally high-status cities and in many cases out of existing cities altogether, so that all destinations became equivalent and local supply was no longer the norm. The rise of empires gave these industrial producers access to political power that previously would have only been associated with social status. Exercising this political power led to legal protections of these industrial producers' and distributors' new-found rights.

As a consequence, by the end of the Victorian era, the industrial world was firmly set on a model of hubs and spokes: The hubs were sources of production that could control supply and creation of wealth, while the spokes -- channels of distribution and communication -- were control points but also allowed the influence of the hubs to be extended to a great distance. This topology was effective in growing the well-being of society at large and generating immense wealth for those owning the control points, thus protecting them both in culture, and in law.

That law included an evolution of earlier ideas that a temporary monopoly was a way to encourage innovators to share their innovations with society at large, to stimulate the advance of the "standing on the shoulders of giants" effect. While the ideas of copyright and patents had their roots in earlier generations, the hub-and-spoke topology of the industrial era was especially well suited to protection using these "intellectual monopolies", providing clear rights and tough sanctions to govern the robust competition between the new barons of commerce. Both copyrights and patents were understood as a temporary monopoly for the creator of goods to permit successful commerce while also forcing those benefiting from them to share their creative works and know-how freely with society at large, adding new richness to what's now called "the public commons".

The balance between commercial success and the growth of the commons was crucial. Too much emphasis on the former would allow a few individuals to become immensely rich while protected from fair competition; too much emphasis on the latter would lead to producers keeping secrets and crippling progress for society as a whole. Over time, with notable legal cases as exemplars, the rules around copyrights and patents evolved to where they were very well-suited to the industrial society. Naturally the balance was constantly tested -- entrepreneurs are constantly looking for clever ways to exploit both loopholes and innovations to make money -- but it's fair to say that by the middle of the 20th century the hub-and-spoke topology was stable and effective, even in the shadow of two world wars.

The industrial revolution created an economy dependent on high-investment mass production, funded by aggregated high-worth investment, monetised via high-volume distribution channels and marketed through one-way mass communication channels. Each step of that economic flow depended on the person controlling the mechanism. Thus, industrial society became a sequence of control points that each new venture aimed back to its hub so that the various spokes fed each success. As a result, arbitration on control points in production, supply and communications evolved into a complex art-form.

As abuses and disasters exposed weaknesses in the system, law was created to regulate them for the public benefit. The system's vectors in law revolved around a group of concepts involving the regulation of monopoly on those control points. While some of the concepts existed before, industrial society repurposed or invented copyright, trademarks, patents and trade secrets to become the projections of the control points. All are very different in what they regulate and how they do it, but for the oligarchy inheriting (or aspiring to inherit) the industrial riches of the 19th and 20th centuries in the 21st century, all are part of the same palette of control that determines who can profit in the marketplace.

It was reasonable on many issues in the passing industrial society for policy makers to consult business leaders who would be affected by their decisions. In those cases, Parliament could often be expected to balance personal needs on behalf of the citizens who elected them. There were also a few issues solely about the interaction of individuals - although increasingly, interested groups with business funding would participate.

Commercial issues are the domain of commercial organisations and thus appropriate for commercial input. As a result, most industries gradually develop a sector for influencing legislation. Indeed, the computer technology industry offered an opportunity to see just such a lobbying activity evolve over the last 30 years. It's expensive, time-consuming and it can easily cause blowback to the public image of corporations pressing to have their proprietary interests preferred by the law. As a result, the natural trajectory of policy engagement moves from direct comment to direct committee engagement to authored position statements to paying for industry consortia to take those actions until, eventually, even those consortia try to hide from public gaze by paying independent experts to provide input to the legislative process on their behalf. In mature lobbying situations, the funding source paying for political results is often so tenuous that it takes focussed and expert research to follow the money back to the sources.

None of this is a mystery in the corridors of power. Politicians respond to this evolution of influence by creating processes that assume its existence and go on to channel it. On new, personal topics, some direct citizen input is expected and perhaps even sought, yet organised pressure groups still come to dominate. But for almost all topics today, the process of influence has evolved to a stage where fully-crafted and cloaked input is assumed to be the norm. Civil servants follow detailed rules to sift and summarise it, and politicians assume a role akin to a judge arbitrating impartially between experts, but do so with an eye to their party's opinion. In this fully evolved state, the citizens' views are irrelevant. Career experts feeding career civil servants provide the data, and career politicians make all the decisions.

As a consequence, all are seen not as the privileged, temporary monopolies they are, given with the consent of society in exchange for enhancement of the common good. Since these 'intellectual monopolies' are all the keys to control points in a supply system designed along the hub-spoke model of the industrial society, and since each key unlocks potential exclusive monetisation, proponents for their beneficiaries refer to these wildly differing privileges as 'property', and collectively as 'intellectual property'. Anyone referring to them in this way is framing the discussion, since we are culturally trained to understand 'property' in particular ways: persistent rather than transient, inalienable rather than collectively granted, tangible rather than ephemeral. This in turn has undesirable side effects, as these cultural instincts bias our thinking ahead of understanding the issues.

The Meshed Society

While society has always hosted individual artisans or groups of artisans, the "creator-consumer" is a new twist on the old, pre-industrial norm. It refers to individuals who at various times create new things and improve existing things ("make"), and collaborate with others to "make" or consume what others "make". No single mode from that trio is preferred, and any given encounter may involve all three. Further, not every engagement involves a monetary transaction. Some might, and most consumption of the work of others will, but there's no given; each instance stands by its own dynamic and rules. While these dynamics have existed before on a local scale in villages all over the world, the Internet creates a "global village" that adds a new, scalable dynamic. As we discover more and more ways to eliminate the mediators and control points in our interactions, society is transformed. It was a series of hubs with privileged interconnections intermediating supply to consumers; it is becoming a constantly shifting mesh of ad-hoc direct interactions -- an "adhocracy", as Alvin Toffler described it.

The ubiquity of the world-wide web changes the rules. In its meshed topology, every participant is a peer and there is no scope for natural control points. In the adhocracy, individuals play the roles of user, repurposer, maker, buyer and collaborator in a constantly changing spectrum of combinations. But the law, gathered as it has around the hub-and-spoke worldview of the industrial society, treats many of these roles as privileged, because they have historically been reserved only for commercial entities. The meshed society finds ways to route around, or circumvent, attempts to introduce artificial control points, and any attempt to introduce them is treated collectively as damage. Hence, 'circumvention' is a crucial marker as well. In the meshed society built on the internet, 'circumvention' describes normal, healthy operation. To prohibit it is to cling to the past.

Take for example copyright extension and the unremitting pressure from content-dependent industries to extend copyright further and further. Seen as a temporary exception to the societal norm that cultural artefacts are universal, copyright seems reasonable to allow an author a limited time to recoup investment in the work. Extending copyright within this frame elicits questions of "why is that needed" and "how does society benefit from that extended isolation of the work from its true status as part of collective culture". But view copyright as property and the frame changes. We see copyright as the ownership of a work by its author, and assume it should be inalienable and persistent as a result.

Extension then becomes the reasonable recognition of the property rights of the author, and collective culture is seen as abandonment. This frame elicits questions of "why not" and "why shouldn't authors be rewarded for their work". Seen as property, copyright violations -- and even resisting the extension of term -- is seen as "theft", a word that's almost impossible to reconcile with the concept of a temporarily granted and ephemeral exclusivity on a work which is in no way eroded by multiple use. In fact, "theft", "steal, "stolen" and the like are all the genetic markers in this context of an apologist for a robber-baron.

Consider these symptoms:

- Penalties for copyright infringement are massively punitive, out of all proportion to any harm, because the law assumes an industrial creator is involved.
- Software patents are pursued rather than prevented, on the assumption that patent infringers must be industrial competitors rather than creative peers.

- There's no balance to content takedown powers of copyright-holders, because the only role of an individual is assumed to be "consumer" so no appeal is considered necessary.
- Discussion of Internet-related legislation places it in the same category as one-way mass media like television, radio and newspapers.
- Legislatures -- and the organisations that feed them -- seeks input on timescales and with methods that assume a location in the capital and an abundance of available daily time.
- Politicians regard e-mails from ordinary citizens in the same light as spam and want to restrict or ignore mass input.

Together they tell a story of the paradigm of the industrial society being abused to stifle the emergence of the meshed society.

Why No One Speaks For Me

These symptoms are linked to the same root cause. All this evolutionary change has yet to be reflected in the legislative process in any country. The Web may be a quarter of a century old, but there's been almost no progress refactoring the legislative process itself, let alone the law, to fit the new, meshed society. Instead, processes continue to assume the control-point-based industrial society is the norm and that the representatives of those control points are the appropriate source of input to deliberations.

But in the meshed society, control points are damage. So the process is now skewed to allow the source of society's problems to have the dominant voice in their solution, rather than the people who are building the citizen-creator-consumer future. Those pioneers easily run afoul of the rules intended to regulate the old world, and the penalties associated are disproportionate with the acts they address: They are designed as disincentives for industrial gaming, not the human-scale actions of the meshed society.

All these things mean that facing the changes of the meshed Internet society by tweaking the rules of the industrial society will inevitably fail; instead, we need to fully refactor those rules to account for the new topology of society, as well as build mechanisms for devising legislation that consider and empower the pioneers of the meshed society. Refactoring means understanding the new dynamics, discovering the modalities of the ways they will be gamed and inventing fair regulation to prevent those games.

Computer industry veteran Simon Phipps has been involved at a strategic level in some of the world's leading technology companies. He worked with OSI standards for Unisys in the eighties, on the first commercial collaborative conferencing software in the nineties, and helped introduce both Java and XML at IBM. He was a key figure in open sourcing Java, Solaris and the rest of Sun Microsystems' software portfolio. In addition to senior leadership positions he has worked in such hands-on roles as field engineer, programmer and systems analyst, as well as run a software publishing company.

In addition to running his own management consulting company, Meshed Insights Ltd, he serves as a Director on the boards of the Open Source Initiative, the Open Rights Group and the MariaDB Foundation and on the advisory board of Open Source for America.

A widely read thought-leader, he publishes regularly both on his own blog and in many other places such as IDG's InfoWorld. He holds a degree in electronic engineering and is a Chartered Engineer and Fellow of the British Computer Society.

His personal home page and blog is http://www.webmink.com

Forking the patent system: Pollyanna in Patent-Land?

By Peter Langley

A powerfully effective system of social organisation. A template for driving widespread, collaborative innovation. Crafted through a complex, multi-expert process of collaborative development. Constantly evolving. Largely above, and indifferent, to the perceptions of ordinary consumers. May fork in interesting ways.

That these attributes apply equally to both patent law and to open source is one of those interesting paradoxes worth reflecting upon for a moment. The orthodoxy is that the systems of patent law and FOSS are conflicting and inevitably mutually exclusive – it is perhaps surprising that so many defining characteristics are common to both. And quite possibly these apparently incompatible systems may converge closer still: In this short essay, we'll examine how patent law might be in the process of forking in ways not only favourable to FOSS, but that excise the tensions between patent law and FOSS as systems for driving innovation. It may prove Pollyanna in Patent-Land, at least in the very near-term. But let's view the world through that lens for a moment and see what it reveals.

We may possibly be at the start of a major fork in the patent system, reflecting two distinct modes of innovation: the first mode, where realising a single innovation is laborious and vastly costly – pharmaceutical innovation, for example, where a single new compound can cost \$500M and 10 years to develop, can generate \$10Bn a year in sales and is protected by a small handful of patents. And the second mode, where innovation is cheap, rapid, incremental and at times effortless and inevitable. Products are affected by thousands, perhaps tens of thousands of patents. For this second mode, one is reminded of Eben Moglen's Metaphorical Corollary to Faraday's Law: 'Wrap the Internet around every brain on the planet and spin the planet. Software flows in the wires. It's an emergent property of human minds to create.' So it is in this second mode that FOSS operates.

Legally, the first mode is characterised by the ready availability of injunctions to stop clone products; and by the possibility of very substantial damages. Patent law has traditionally assumed that injunctions and the possibility of substantial damages is the sine qua non of its existence; treating both modes of innovation in the same manner. But in recent years, we have started to discern an understanding that these different modes of innovation should just possibly be treated differently in legal terms – that where innovation is cheap, rapid, and incremental (i.e. where FOSS plays) then injunctions might possibly be much harder to obtain, and damages should be very low. If patent law evolves in this direction (and evolution in law can be as halting, unsure and provisional as it is elsewhere), then patent law will not only cease to pose the existential threat it currently poses to FOSS, but may bring itself into alignment with FOSS' ultimate goals of promoting the open and co-operative sharing of innovation. FOSS may then find that it can co-exist quite happily enough within a forked patent system.

We'll look now at some of the specifics. First, injunctions. In recent US patent litigation, the grant of an injunction requires proof of a sufficiently strong causal nexus relating the alleged harm to the alleged infringement – which typically requires showing that consumers buy the infringing product 'because it is equipped with the apparatus claimed in the patent and not merely because it includes a feature of the type covered by the patent' [115]).

For many cases involving FOSS, this causal nexus may well prove to be exceptionally difficult to establish. Consider, for example, a specific kernel function allegedly covered by a patent – could one in practice adduce compelling evidence that consumers buy say a mobile phone solely because it has that specific kernel function? If not, then an injunction may not be available. This approach leaves entirely open the possibility of injunctions to prevent copying of a feature that is genuinely so exceptional and significant that consumers buy the smartphone specifically because of it – but as smartphones continue their evolutionary path as multi-function tools, capable of doing thousands of different tasks, the possibility of the emergence of a single new and patented function that overwhelmingly drives consumers purchasing behaviour seems not only remote but also fast-receding. A radical new capability like 3D holographic real-time imaging would suffice – but I'd struggle to identify anything in say the kernel that would meet this standard. So for most FOSS developers, the injunctive risk is both distant and diminishing.

That Apple was denied an injunction[116] against Samsung, despite the 21 August 2012 jury returning a verdict of infringement, shows how difficult in practice meeting the causal nexus standard can be. The US Court of Appeals for the Federal Circuit will hear Apple's appeal from this judgement in mid 2013; no-doubt, a defining moment of the Smartphone Wars, and

---

[115] The Federal Circuit's Apple II opinion: Apple, Inc v Samsung Electronics Co., Ltd 695 F.3d 1370 1374 1376 (Fed Cir 2012)

[116] See order Denying Motion for Permanent Injunction, Apple, Inc v Samsung Electronics Co., Ltd Case No. 11-CV-01846-LHK, on appeal to the Federal Circuit as of early 2013

developing patent jurisprudence too. If the Federal Circuit supports the rigorous application of the causal nexus text to injunctions, then the fork will be real and solid: one fork for the first mode of innovation, where causal nexus can generally be established and so injunctions will be available, and another fork covering much of the software space where FOSS plays, where causal nexus will be exceptionally hard to prove and so injunctions will in practice not be available – a highly attractive outcome for FOSS.

Another important theme, supplementing the highly attractive causal nexus test for injunctions, is the developing jurisprudence around the 'public interest'. See[117] for example: "the public interest does not support removing phones from the market when the infringing components constitute such limited parts of complex, multi-faceted products". The broad application of this approach by the courts to software will again make it far harder for much of the areas where FOSS operates to be targeted. See also Justice Kennedy's concurring opinion in the US Supreme Court judgement eBay[118]: 'when the patented invention is but a small component of the product the companies seek to produce and the threat of an injunction is employed simply for undue leverage in negotiations, legal damages may well be sufficient to compensate for infringement and an injunction may not serve the public interest.'

Another key issue in all patent litigation is the identity of the royalty base: is the % royalty rate sought (typically in the 1% to

---

[117] See order Denying Motion for Permanent Injunction, Apple, Inc v Samsung Electronics Co., Ltd Case No. 11-CV-01846-LHK, on appeal to the Federal Circuit as of early 2013

[118] eBay Inc v Merc Exchange, LLC 547 US 388 (2006)

2% range for software patent litigation) to be applied to the entire market value of say a smartphone, or should it be applied to a component, such as a chip in the device? Invariably and unsurprisingly, patent holders seeking royalties will base their demands on the entire market value of the end product, since it is the most valuable element in the chain of commerce, even though their patents might cover features which are relevant to just a single component in the device (perhaps the processor) and there are hundreds of other components in the final product.

The US position is both tolerably clear, and favourable to FOSS, with the most recent case from the Federal Circuit, LaserDynamics v. Quanta, holding[119]:

> We reaffirm that in any case involving multi-component products, patentees may not calculate damages based on sales of the entire product, as opposed to the smallest saleable patent practicing unit, without showing that the demand for the entire product is attributable to the patented feature.

So, when attacking FOSS functions, patent holders will face substantial challenges meeting this evidentiary burden, which mirrors the causal nexus standard relevant to injunctions. Further, even if they can establish sufficient proof that their patented feature drives demand, in many cases, the 'smallest saleable unit' for software patents will be the chip or chip+ROM module in the accused products, or code itself, and that will be priced at a small fraction of the final consumer item.

---

[119]   http://www.cafc.uscourts.gov/images/stories/opinions-orders/ 11-1440-1470.pdf

Let's now imagine a patent infringement case covering a relatively minor software function. The function is something that (like most patented software functions) can be invented-around. What theory should we apply to working out the fair compensation to the patent holder for the infringement? One possible argument, suggested by Judge Posner in his highly influential Opinion and Order dismissing with prejudice patent suits brought by Apple and Microsoft,[120] is to say that compensation for the major software company is 'royalties capped at the minimum design-around costs' since that equates to what a prudent infringer would have paid to secure a license. Invent-around costs may be small and possibly close to zero when the FOSS community collaborates to design or invent-around a software patent. Then, on Judge Posner's theory, the damages due, even when a FOSS function is held to infringe, would be minimal.

A Quick Re-cap

Injunctions in the US may require the patent holder to prove a causal nexus between the patented feature and the demand – but this will often be hard to prove with software patents impacting FOSS;

The royalty base when assessing damages may, in the US, be the smallest saleable unit and not the entire market value (e.g. entire costs of a smartphone) where it cannot be proven the patented feature drives the demand. With patents that may impact FOSS, the royalty base would typically then be a chip programmed with the code that implements the patented feature.

---

[120] See Opinion and Order of June 22, 2012, Apple, Inc. and next Software Inc., v Motorola, Inc., and Motorola Mobility, Inc., Case No. 1:11-cv-08540

More speculatively, damages when infringement is found may be based on the costs associated with inventing-around - which may well be close to zero for FOSS.

Judicially led reform transformative forking of the patent system, in ways largely favourable to FOSS, would be an attractive irony. Wars, even patent wars, can lead to surprising and unexpected consequences.

Peter Langley is the founder and managing director of Origin. Peter has a degree in physics and is a Solicitor of the Supreme Court of England & Wales, a Patent Attorney and a Trade Mark Attorney. He has been voted one of the top 40 technology lawyers in the UK.

Peter has advised many leading technology companies, including TomTom, TeleAtlas, ARM, Sharp, Symbian and Unilever, as well as VCs and start-ups. He focuses on IP litigation, IP strategy and branding; he also has extensive experience in protecting software. He has handled patents in the following areas: GPS sat nav, digital mapping, semiconductors, encryption, compact disc, mobile telephony, 3G, LTE, WI-Max, femtocell, real-time holography, mobile device operating systems, mobile device UX, video compression, anti-tamper software, website optimisation, cloud-based music systems, LCDs, voice recognition, FX trading, systematic trading algorithms and wave energy systems.

He and his team have managed major patent litigation in the US (including S337 ITC proceedings), Germany, Japan, Netherlands, and the UK; ICC arbitration in the UK and Switzerland; resolved global IP disputes through mediation; acquired over $40M in patents for various clients in recent years; and negotiated IP cross-licenses with many of the major rights holders in the wireless, electronics and software sectors.

He is Visiting Professorial Fellow in Law at the Centre for Digital Music, Queen Mary College, London University.

Learn More

Useful Links

To learn more about OpenForum Europe visit:
http://www.openforumeurope.org

To learn more about OpenForum Academy visit:
http://www.openforumacademy.org

To learn more about Open Innovation visit:
http://www.openforumacademy.org/library

This book is released under an open license. Please feel free to share it in printed or digital form with anyone you believe would find it useful.

www.ingramcontent.com/pod-product-compliance
Lightning Source LLC
Chambersburg PA
CBHW032020170526
45157CB00002B/789

* 9 7 8 1 3 0 4 0 1 5 5 1 8 *